SHARIA MEETS SECULAR CONSTITUTION

ISLAMIC LAW IN INDEPEDENT INDIA

MUBASHIR VATTAPARAMBAN

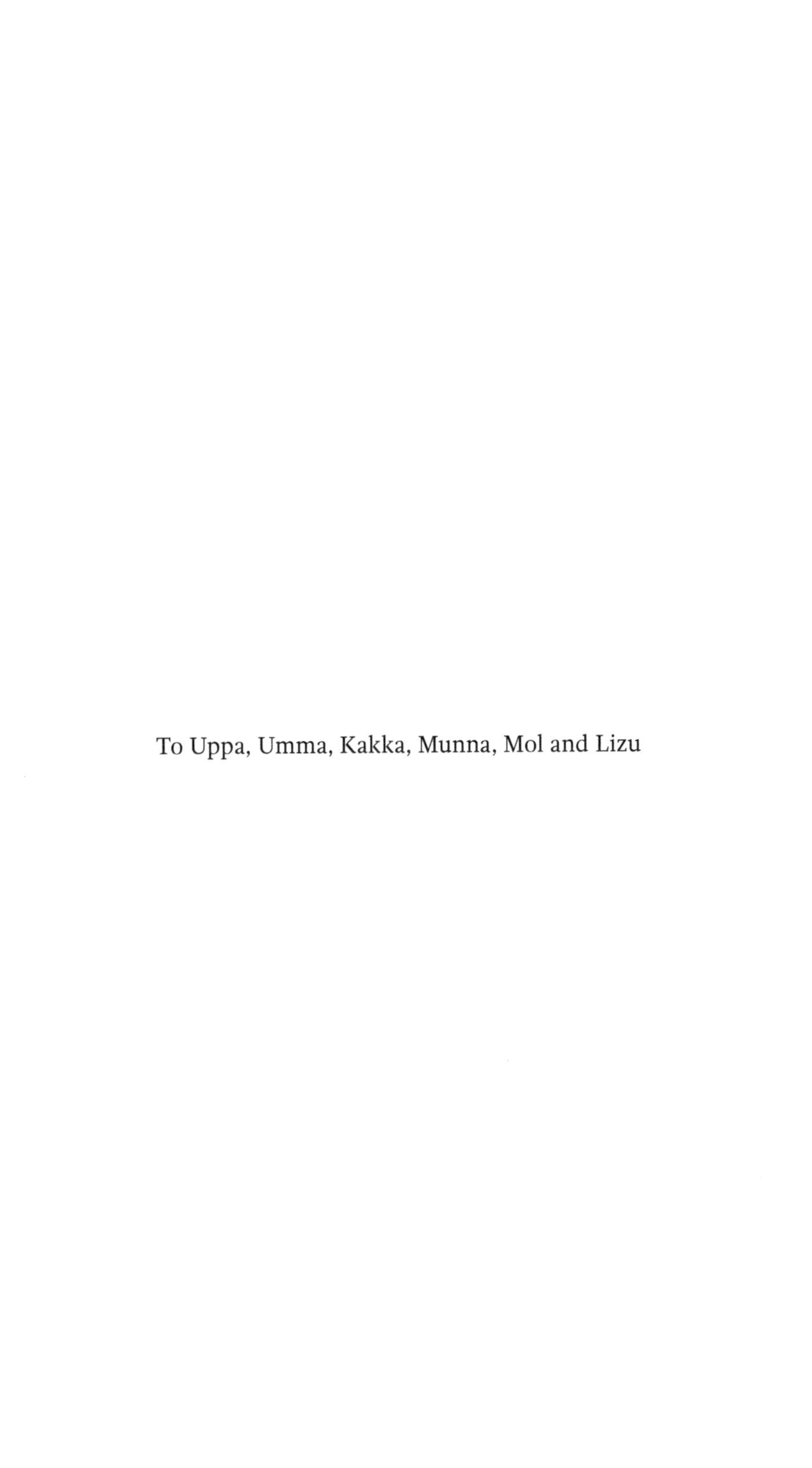

To Uppa, Umma, Kakka, Munna, Mol and Lizu

Contents

Contents

Foreword

In the ever-evolving landscape of modern India, the interaction between Islamic Sharia and the secular constitution presents a complex and nuanced relationship. This dynamic has shaped, and continues to shape, the socio-political discourse of the nation. As the Head of the Department of Islamic Studies at Jamia Millia Islamia, it is with great pleasure and a sense of responsibility that I write the foreword to Sharia Meets Constitution: Islamic Sharia in Independent India, a compilation of the insightful articles authored by Mubashir Vattaparamban.

The book before you is not just a collection of articles; it is a profound exploration of the intersection between faith and the law, tradition and modernity, and the individual and the state. Each chapter meticulously unpacks the challenges, opportunities, and intricacies involved in the coexistence of Islamic Sharia within the framework of India's secular constitution.

Mubashir Vattaparamban, through his scholarly work, provides an essential contribution to our understanding of how Islamic jurisprudence has adapted to the legal and constitutional framework of an independent India. His articles delve into the historical evolution of Sharia in the Indian context, the impact of colonialism, and the subsequent struggles and adaptations that have taken place in post-colonial India.

One of the key strengths of this book is its ability to present complex legal and religious concepts in a manner that is both accessible and thought-provoking. The author's deep understanding of both Islamic law and the Indian legal system allows him to present a balanced and informed perspective on the subject. Through his work, readers are invited to engage with questions of identity, rights, and the role of religion in a secular state.

As we navigate the 21st century, the themes discussed in this book are more relevant than ever. The relationship between religious laws and the secular state is a topic of significant debate, not just in India, but across the world. This book offers a crucial perspective on how these issues have been addressed in India, a country known for its religious diversity and commitment to secularism.

I am confident that Sharia Meets Constitution: Islamic Sharia in Independent India will serve as a valuable resource for scholars, students, and anyone interested in the interplay between religion and law in India. Mubashir Vattaparamban's work will undoubtedly contribute to ongoing discussions and encourage further research in this critical area of study.

I commend the author for his dedication and scholarship, and I am certain that this book will be an important addition to the academic discourse on Islamic Sharia and the Indian Constitution.

Preface

The interaction between Islamic Sharia and secular constitutional frameworks is a subject of profound significance, particularly in a diverse and pluralistic society like India. The tension between these two systems of law—one rooted in religious tradition and the other in secular governance—reflects broader global debates about the role of religion in public life, the scope of personal freedom, and the meaning of justice in a modern society. In this book, we delve into these complex issues, exploring the historical, legal, and social dimensions of Sharia law as it intersects with India's secular constitution.

India's experience with Islamic law is unique, shaped by centuries of coexistence between different religious communities under a single political framework. The Indian Constitution, which guarantees freedom of religion while upholding a secular state, provides a fascinating case study of how Sharia has been integrated into a broader legal system that is not explicitly Islamic. This integration, however, has not been without challenges. The coexistence of Sharia with secular laws has led to ongoing debates about the scope of religious freedom, the rights of women and minorities, and the nature of legal pluralism in a democratic society.

The historical roots of Sharia in India can be traced back to the arrival of Islam in the subcontinent, which brought with it a rich tradition of legal scholarship and jurisprudence. Islamic law in India evolved over centuries, adapting to local customs and the political realities of various empires, from the Delhi Sultanate to the Mughal Empire. During the colonial period, British rulers codified aspects of Islamic law, particularly in the realm of personal status laws, which govern marriage, divorce, inheritance, and other family matters. This codification was a double-edged sword: it preserved certain aspects of Sharia while also freezing its development, making it difficult to adapt to changing social conditions.

The post-colonial period saw India emerging as a secular republic, with a constitution that sought to balance the rights of religious communities with the principles of equality and justice. The framers of the Indian Constitution were acutely aware of the diversity of the country and the need to protect religious freedoms while preventing discrimination. This delicate balance is reflected in the inclusion of provisions that allow for the continuation of personal laws based on religious traditions, including Sharia, alongside a uniform civil code that applies to all citizens.

However, the coexistence of Sharia with secular law has not been without controversy. Critics argue that certain aspects of Islamic personal law, particularly in the areas of marriage, divorce, and inheritance, are inconsistent with the principles of gender equality enshrined in the Indian Constitution. These critiques have led to calls for reform, both from within the Muslim community and from broader civil society. At the same time, there are those who defend the continuation of Sharia as an essential aspect of religious freedom, arguing that any attempt to reform Islamic law must come from within the community itself, rather than being imposed by the state.

This book explores these debates in depth, examining the legal, social, and political dimensions of Sharia in contemporary India. We begin with a historical overview of Islamic law in India, tracing its evolution from the pre-colonial period to the present day. We then turn to the challenges and opportunities of integrating Sharia into a secular legal framework, focusing on key issues such as gender equality, minority rights, and legal pluralism. Throughout, we seek to provide a nuanced understanding of the complexities of Sharia in India, recognizing both its importance to the Muslim community and the challenges it poses in a secular state.

One of the central themes of this book is the tension between tradition and modernity. Islamic law, like any legal system, is not static; it has evolved over time in response to changing social, political, and economic conditions. However, the process of legal reform within the framework of Sharia is often slow and contested, particularly when it comes to issues that touch on deeply held religious beliefs. In India, this tension is particularly acute, as the country grapples with the demands of a modern, pluralistic society while respecting the religious traditions of its diverse population.

The role of women in Islamic law is a particularly contentious issue, and one that we explore in depth in this book. Critics of Sharia often point to the unequal treatment of women in areas such as divorce, inheritance, and custody as evidence that Islamic law is incompatible with modern principles of gender equality. However, this critique overlooks the fact that there is a wide range of opinions within the Muslim community about the interpretation and application of Sharia, with many scholars and activists advocating for reforms that would bring Islamic law in line with contemporary standards of justice and equality. This book examines these debates, highlighting the diversity of views within the Muslim community and the ways in which Islamic law is being reinterpreted and reformed in response to changing social conditions.

Another important theme of this book is the concept of legal pluralism—the idea that multiple legal systems can coexist within a single state. India is one of the few countries in the world where personal laws based on religious traditions are recognized alongside a secular legal system. This legal pluralism is both a strength and a challenge. On the one hand, it allows for the accommodation of religious diversity and the protection of minority rights. On the other hand, it can lead to inconsistencies and conflicts between different legal systems, particularly when it comes to issues of gender equality and social justice. This book explores the complexities of legal pluralism in India, examining both the benefits and the challenges of maintaining a system in which Sharia coexists with secular law.

Ultimately, this book seeks to provide a comprehensive and balanced analysis of the role of Sharia in contemporary India. We recognize the importance of Islamic law to the Muslim community, while also acknowledging the challenges it poses in a secular state committed to principles of equality and justice. Our goal is not to take sides in the debates about Sharia but rather to provide readers with a deeper understanding of the issues at stake and the ways in which these issues are being addressed in India today.

In conclusion, the book is a timely and important contribution to the ongoing debates about the role of religion in public life, the meaning of justice in a pluralistic society, and the challenges of integrating religious traditions into a secular legal framework. We hope that this book will serve as a valuable resource for scholars, policymakers, and anyone interested in the complex relationship between Islamic law and secular governance in India.

Acknowledgements

Writing this book has been a journey of discovery, growth, and perseverance, and it would not have been possible without the unwavering support, encouragement, and guidance of many people. I would like to take this opportunity to express my deepest gratitude to those who have stood by me throughout this process.

First and foremost, I would like to thank my family. To my parents, your unconditional love, belief in my abilities, and constant encouragement have been the bedrock upon which I have built my aspirations. Your support has given me the strength to pursue my passion for writing and the determination to see this project through to completion. To my siblings, thank you for your understanding, patience, and the countless ways you have been there for me, especially during the challenging times.

To my friends, who have been a source of inspiration, joy, and comfort throughout this journey, I am incredibly grateful. Your words of encouragement, late-night discussions, and willingness to listen to my ideas have fueled my creativity and kept me motivated. Thank you for being my sounding boards, my critics, and my cheerleaders. Your friendship has meant the world to me.

I would also like to extend my heartfelt thanks to my teachers and mentors, whose wisdom, guidance, and expertise have been instrumental in shaping my thinking and approach to this work. Your teachings have not only expanded my knowledge but have also instilled in me a deep sense of curiosity and a commitment to lifelong learning. Thank you for pushing me to think critically, to question, and to strive for excellence. Your influence is reflected in every page of this book.

Finally, I want to acknowledge everyone who has contributed to this project in ways big and small. Whether through offering feedback, sharing resources, or simply providing a word of encouragement, your support has been invaluable. This book is as much yours as it is mine, and I am deeply thankful for your presence in my life.

To all of you, from the bottom of my heart, thank you.

THEORETICAL CONTEXT

CHAPTER I

Sharia In New Millennium

Islamic law, known as Sharia, represents a comprehensive legal system derived from the Quran, the Hadith (the sayings and actions of Prophet Muhammad), and centuries of jurisprudence. Sharia governs not only religious rituals but also aspects of day-to-day life, including family law, finance, contracts, and criminal justice. Sharia is interpreted through Fiqh, or Islamic jurisprudence, which has given rise to various schools of thought.

Before the advent of colonialism, Islamic law was the dominant legal system in many Muslim-majority regions. It was deeply integrated into the social, economic, and political fabric of these societies. Islamic legal scholars, known as Ulema, played a central role in interpreting and applying Sharia, ensuring that it remained relevant to the needs of the Muslim community.

The Impact Of Colonialism On Islamic Legal Traditions

The colonial era marked a significant disruption in the development of Islamic law. European colonial powers, particularly Britain and France, introduced their legal systems into the colonies, often relegating Sharia to matters of personal status law. This imposition created a dual legal system, where Islamic law coexisted with, and was often overshadowed by, Western legal frameworks.

Purpose and Scope of the Article This article aims to explore the evolution of Islamic law in the modern post-colonial world. It examines how colonialism altered the trajectory of Islamic legal traditions, the challenges and opportunities faced by Islamic law in contemporary Muslim-majority societies, and the ongoing struggle to balance traditional Islamic principles with modern legal and political realities.

Historical Overview 0f Islamic Law

Early Development of Islamic Law Islamic law began to take shape during the lifetime of Prophet Muhammad and continued

3

to develop after his death. The Quran, as the primary source of Islamic law, provides the foundational principles, while the Hadith supplements it with detailed guidance on various issues. As Islam spread across the Arabian Peninsula and beyond, Islamic law evolved to address the diverse needs of a growing Muslim community.

Major Schools of Thought The development of Islamic jurisprudence led to the emergence of several schools of thought, each with its own interpretation of Sharia. In Sunni Islam, the four main schools are Hanafi, Maliki, Shafi'i, and Hanbali, while Shia Islam primarily follows the Ja'fari school. These schools differ in their methods of interpreting the Quran and Hadith, as well as in their views on various legal issues.

The Role of Islamic Law in Pre-Colonial Muslim Societies Before the colonial era, Islamic law was the primary legal framework in many Muslim-majority regions. Sharia governed all aspects of life, including governance, trade, family, and criminal justice. Islamic courts were the main institutions for legal adjudication, and the Ulema held significant authority in society.

Colonial Interventions and Legal Reforms The arrival of European colonial powers in the Muslim world brought about significant changes in the legal landscape. Colonial administrators introduced Western legal systems, which often conflicted with traditional Islamic practices. In some cases, colonial authorities codified Islamic law, reducing its flexibility and adapting it to fit colonial objectives. These interventions laid the groundwork for the legal dualism seen in many post-colonial Muslim societies.

Impact Of Colonialism On Islamic Law

Legal Dualism: The Introduction of Western Legal Systems Colonial powers established dual legal systems in their colonies, where Western law was applied to matters of governance, commerce, and criminal justice, while Islamic law was confined to personal status issues such as marriage, divorce, and inheritance. This division undermined the authority of Islamic law and marginalized the Ulema.

Codification of Laws: Civil, Criminal, and Family Law In an effort to control and simplify legal processes, colonial authorities often codified Islamic law. This process involved translating Sharia into written codes, which were then applied in colonial courts. However, this codification stripped Islamic law of its traditional interpretative flexibility, leading to a more rigid and often distorted application of Sharia principles.

The Decline of Sharia Courts and the Rise of Secular Courts As colonial powers expanded their control over Muslim-majority regions, they established secular courts that operated alongside or in place of traditional Sharia courts. These secular courts were staffed by colonial officials and often applied Western legal principles, further eroding the influence of Islamic law.

Colonial Legacies in Post-Colonial Legal Systems The legal systems established during the colonial period have had a lasting impact on post-colonial Muslim societies. Many countries retained the dual legal system, with Islamic law confined to personal status matters. In some cases, post-colonial governments continued to codify Islamic law, often using it as a tool for political control rather than as a reflection of religious principles.

Post-Colonial Reassertion Of Islamic Law

Revivalism and Reform Movements The post-colonial period saw a resurgence of interest in Islamic law, driven by revivalist and reform movements. These movements, such as Salafism, Wahhabism, and the Muslim Brotherhood, sought to reassert the role of Sharia in governance and society, often in opposition to the secular legal frameworks inherited from colonialism.

The Role of Islamic Law in National Identity and State-Building In many post-colonial Muslim countries, Islamic law became a key component of national identity and state-building efforts. Leaders sought to legitimize their authority by invoking Sharia, while also using Islamic law as a means of unifying diverse populations and asserting independence from former colonial powers.

Islamic Constitutions and Legal Pluralism Some post-colonial states adopted constitutions that enshrined Islamic law as the supreme legal authority, while others maintained a pluralistic legal system that incorporated both Sharia and secular law. These different approaches reflect the complex relationship between religion and state in the post-colonial Muslim world.

Pakistan: Following independence, Pakistan adopted a legal system that blends Islamic and secular law. However, the role of Sharia has been a contentious issue, with periodic efforts to impose stricter interpretations of Islamic law.

Sudan: Sudan has experienced several shifts in its legal system, with periods of strict Sharia enforcement followed by more secular approaches. The application of Islamic law has been a central issue in the country's political conflicts.

Iran: The 1979 Islamic Revolution led to the establishment of a theocratic state in Iran, where Islamic law is the foundation of the legal system. The Iranian model represents one of the most comprehensive applications of Sharia in the modern world.

Contemporary Challenges In the Application of Islamic Law

The Tension Between Universal Human Rights and Islamic Law One of the most significant challenges facing Islamic law in the modern world is the perceived tension between Sharia and universal human rights. Issues such as freedom of religion, gender equality, and the rights of minorities are often seen as conflicting with traditional interpretations of Islamic law.

Women's Rights and Gender Equality The status of women under Islamic law has been a focal point of debate in both Muslim and non-Muslim societies. Critics argue that certain interpretations of Sharia restrict women's rights, particularly in areas such as inheritance, divorce, and legal testimony. However, there are also movements within the Muslim world advocating for more gender-equitable interpretations of Islamic law.

Minority Rights in Muslim-Majority Countries In some Muslim-majority countries, non-Muslim minorities face legal and social discrimination under Islamic law. Issues such as religious conversion, blasphemy, and interfaith marriages are often contentious, leading to calls for legal reforms that would better protect minority rights.

The Role of Islamic Law in Globalized Legal Frameworks As Muslim-majority countries increasingly participate in global legal frameworks, there is a growing need to reconcile Islamic law with international legal standards. This challenge is particularly evident in areas such as international human rights law, trade law, and counter-terrorism efforts.

Islamic Law And Global Politics

The Use of Islamic Law in International Relations Islamic law plays a significant role in the foreign policies of some Muslim-majority countries. For example, Sharia principles influence diplomatic relations, particularly with non-Muslim states, and are often invoked in discussions of international justice and human rights.

The Influence of Islamic Law in International Organizations Organizations such as the Organization of Islamic Cooperation (OIC) promote the application of Islamic law in international affairs. The OIC, for instance, advocates for the protection of Muslim minorities worldwide and the recognition of Islamic legal principles in global governance.

Sharia and Counter-Terrorism Policies In the post-9/11 world, the relationship between Islamic law and counter-terrorism has become a major issue. Some governments have used Sharia to justify counter-terrorism measures, while others have sought to reform Islamic law to counter extremist ideologies.

The Role of Islamic Finance in the Global Economy Islamic finance, which operates in accordance with Sharia principles, has become an important part of the global financial system. Islamic banks and financial institutions adhere to rules prohibiting interest (riba) and speculative investments, which has attracted both Muslim and non-Muslim investors seeking ethical alternatives to conventional finance.

Case Studies Of Islamic Law In Modern States

Saudi Arabia: Strict Application of Sharia in Governance and Society Saudi Arabia represents one of the most rigorous applications of Islamic law in the modern world. The country's legal system is based entirely on Sharia, and religious authorities wield significant power in both legal and political matters. This strict adherence to Sharia has implications for issues such as gender rights, criminal justice, and religious freedom.

Malaysia: A Dual Legal System Balancing Sharia and Civil Law Malaysia has a unique legal system that incorporates both Islamic and civil law. Sharia courts in Malaysia handle matters related to family law and personal status for Muslims, while civil courts deal with other legal issues. This dual system reflects Malaysia's multicultural society and the government's efforts to balance Islamic principles with secular governance.

Nigeria: Regional Application of Sharia in a Secular Federal State In Nigeria, Sharia is applied in the northern states, where Muslims are the majority, while the southern states follow secular law. This regional application of Islamic law has led to tensions and conflicts, particularly in areas where the population is religiously diverse.

Egypt: The Role of Al-Azhar and the Judiciary in Interpreting Islamic Law Egypt's legal system is influenced by both Islamic and civil law. Al-Azhar University, one of the oldest and most prestigious Islamic institutions, plays a key role in interpreting Sharia and advising the government on religious matters. However, the Egyptian judiciary also incorporates elements of secular law, leading to a complex legal landscape.

The Future Of Islamic Law In A Post-Colonial World

Trends in the Reformation and Modernization of Islamic Law There is an ongoing debate within the Muslim world about how to reform and modernize Islamic law. Some scholars and activists advocate for a return to the original sources of Sharia, while others call for a more progressive interpretation that aligns with contemporary values and human rights.

The Potential for Harmonizing Islamic and Western Legal Principles As globalization continues to bring different legal systems into contact, there is potential for harmonizing Islamic and Western legal principles. This could involve finding common ground on issues such as human rights, democracy, and the rule of law, while respecting the cultural and religious differences that underpin Islamic legal traditions.

The Role of Education and Scholarship in the Evolution of Islamic Law The future of Islamic law will depend largely on education and scholarship. Islamic legal scholars, or Ulema, have a crucial role to play in interpreting Sharia for the modern world. There is also a growing need for interdisciplinary scholarship that bridges the gap between Islamic and Western legal traditions. The future of Islamic law in the post-colonial world is uncertain and will be shaped by a range of factors, including political developments, social change, and the ongoing dialogue between tradition and modernity. While Islamic law continues to be a source of identity and guidance for many Muslims, it must also adapt to the realities of the modern world if it is to remain relevant and effective.

CHAPTER II

New Theoretical And Theological Developments In Islamic Law Across The Globe

Islamic law, or Sharia, has a rich tradition that has evolved over centuries, adapting to changing social, political, and cultural contexts. In the 21st century, Islamic legal thought has witnessed significant developments, driven by the forces of modernity, globalization, and the rise of new theological interpretations. This article explores these new theoretical and theological developments in Islamic law, focusing on key themes, regional differences, and the impact of contemporary challenges.

Islamic law, traditionally derived from the Quran, Hadith, Ijma (consensus), and Qiyas (analogical reasoning), has been a cornerstone of Muslim societies. The classical schools of jurisprudence (Hanafi, Maliki, Shafi'i, and Hanbali) provided frameworks for interpreting and applying Sharia in diverse contexts. Over time, Islamic law has faced challenges from colonialism, the rise of nation-states, and the encounter with Western legal systems.

The Influence Of Modernity

The advent of modernity has had a profound impact on Islamic law. Modernity introduced new concepts such as human rights, democracy, and secularism, which have challenged traditional interpretations of Sharia. This section explores how Islamic legal thought has responded to these challenges, focusing on key figures and movements that have sought to reconcile Islamic law with modern values.

1. Reformist Movements

Reformist movements within Islam have sought to reinterpret traditional Islamic law to align with modern values. Thinkers like

Muhammad Abduh and Rashid Rida in the late 19th and early 20th centuries emphasized the need for ijtihad (independent reasoning) to address contemporary issues. This legacy continues today, with scholars advocating for gender equality, religious freedom, and human rights within an Islamic framework.

2. Neo-Traditionalism

In contrast to reformists, neo-traditionalists seek to preserve the classical interpretations of Islamic law while adapting them to modern contexts. This approach emphasizes the importance of following established legal methodologies and respecting the authority of traditional scholars. Neo-traditionalists often engage in dialogue with modernist thinkers to find common ground.

3. Salafism and Islamic Law

Salafism, a movement that seeks to return to the practices of the "pious predecessors" (Salaf), has also influenced contemporary Islamic legal thought. Salafi scholars advocate for a strict adherence to the Quran and Hadith, rejecting what they perceive as innovations (bid'ah) in Islamic law. However, within Salafism, there is a spectrum of thought, with some scholars engaging with modernity more than others.

Theological Developments

Theological developments in Islamic law have been shaped by debates over the sources of authority, the role of reason, and the nature of divine will. This section explores key theological trends that have influenced Islamic legal thought in recent decades.

1. The Revival of Maqasid al-Sharia (Objectives of Sharia)

The concept of Maqasid al-Sharia, which refers to the objectives or higher purposes of Islamic law, has gained renewed attention in contemporary Islamic thought. Scholars like Jasser Auda and Mohammad Hashim Kamali have emphasized the importance of understanding the underlying purposes of Sharia, such as justice, mercy, and the common good. This approach allows for a more flexible and context-sensitive application of Islamic law.

2. Reinterpretation of Traditional Sources

Some contemporary scholars have called for a reexamination of traditional sources of Islamic law, arguing that certain interpretations are no longer applicable in the modern context. This has led to debates over the role of Hadith, the use of qiyas, and the relevance of classical legal schools. These debates have sparked new interpretations of issues such as gender relations, minority rights, and economic justice.

3. The Role of Ethics in Islamic Law

Ethical considerations have become increasingly important in contemporary Islamic legal thought. Scholars have explored the relationship between Islamic ethics (Akhlaq) and legal rulings, arguing that ethical principles should guide the interpretation and application of Islamic law. This has led to new discussions on bioethics, environmental ethics, and the ethical dimensions of governance and social justice.

Regional Developments

Islamic law has evolved differently in various regions, influenced by local cultures, politics, and historical contexts. This section examines how new theoretical and theological developments in Islamic law have manifested in different parts of the world.

1. The Middle East and North Africa

In the Middle East and North Africa (MENA) region, Islamic law has been deeply intertwined with state governance. Recent developments include the incorporation of Islamic principles into constitutions and legal systems, as well as debates over the role of Sharia in public life. In countries like Egypt, Tunisia, and Morocco, there have been significant efforts to reform personal status laws, particularly concerning women's rights and family law.

2. South Asia

South Asia, home to a large Muslim population, has seen vibrant debates over Islamic law, particularly in India, Pakistan, and Bangladesh. The region has witnessed the rise of movements advocating for the reform of Muslim personal law, especially concerning gender justice. Additionally, the influence of Sufism and local customs has shaped unique interpretations of Islamic law in this region.

3. Southeast Asia

In Southeast Asia, Islamic law has been influenced by local traditions and the pluralistic nature of societies. Countries like Indonesia and Malaysia have developed hybrid legal systems that incorporate both Islamic and civil law. Recent developments include debates over the implementation of Sharia in areas like Aceh, Indonesia, and the role of Islamic law in a multicultural society.

4. Western Countries

In Western countries, the Muslim diaspora has faced challenges in applying Islamic law within secular legal systems. Issues such as marriage, divorce, and inheritance have led to the development of parallel legal frameworks, such as Sharia councils in the UK. Additionally, the rise of Islamophobia and debates over religious freedom have influenced discussions on the compatibility of Islamic law with Western values.

Contemporary Challenges

The new theoretical and theological developments in Islamic law have been shaped by contemporary challenges, including globalization, technological advancements, and the rise of new social movements. This section explores how these challenges have influenced Islamic legal thought.

1. Globalization and Transnationalism

Globalization has facilitated the exchange of ideas and the spread of Islamic thought across borders. This has led to the emergence of transnational Islamic movements and the development of global networks of scholars and activists. These networks have contributed to the dissemination of new interpretations of Islamic law and the creation of a global Islamic public sphere.

2. Technological Advancements

The rise of digital technology and social media has transformed the way Islamic legal knowledge is produced and disseminated.

Online platforms have enabled scholars and laypeople to engage in discussions on Islamic law, leading to the democratization of religious authority. Additionally, new technologies have raised ethical questions that require fresh interpretations of Islamic law, such as issues related to bioengineering, artificial intelligence, and cybersecurity.

3. Social Movements and Islamic Law

The rise of social movements advocating for gender equality, LGBTQ rights, and environmental justice has challenged traditional interpretations of Islamic law. These movements have prompted scholars to reconsider legal rulings on issues such as marriage, family, and environmental stewardship. The intersection of Islamic law with social justice has become a key area of debate in contemporary Islamic thought.

The new theoretical and theological developments in Islamic law across the globe reflect a dynamic and evolving tradition that continues to adapt to contemporary challenges. While debates over the interpretation and application of Islamic law are ongoing, there is a growing recognition of the need for a more flexible, context-sensitive approach that aligns with modern values and ethical principles. As Islamic law continues to evolve, it will play a crucial role in shaping the future of Muslim societies and their engagement with the wider world.

CHAPTER III

A Global And Historical Exploration: Legislative Reform In Muslim Family Laws

Muslim family laws have undergone significant transformations over the centuries, shaped by a variety of factors, including colonialism, modernization, globalization, and the unique socio-political landscapes of individual Muslim-majority countries. The evolution of these laws has been driven by the need to balance religious principles with the changing needs of society, leading to numerous legislative reforms across the globe. This essay will explore the historical and global dimensions of legislative reform in Muslim family laws, focusing on key regions and periods, and analyzing the driving forces behind these changes.

Historical Background: The Foundations Of Muslim Family Law

Muslim family law, or personal status law, traditionally derives from Islamic jurisprudence (fiqh), which is based on the Quran, the Hadith (sayings and actions of the Prophet Muhammad), and centuries of scholarly interpretation. The four major Sunni schools of law—Hanafi, Maliki, Shafi'i, and Hanbali—along with the Shia Ja'fari school, have provided diverse interpretations of these texts, leading to variations in the application of family law across different regions.

Historically, Muslim family laws have governed areas such as marriage, divorce, inheritance, and child custody. These laws were not static but evolved in response to changing social conditions. For instance, in the pre-modern Islamic world, the interpretation and application of family laws were often flexible, with local customs and the needs of the community playing a significant role in shaping legal practices.

The Impact Of Colonialism On Muslim Family Law

The advent of colonialism in the 19th and 20th centuries brought about profound changes in Muslim societies, including in the realm of family law. European colonial powers, particularly the British and the French, imposed their legal systems on their colonies, often relegating Muslim family law to a secondary status. In many cases, colonial authorities codified Muslim family laws, freezing them in time and reducing the flexibility that had characterized Islamic jurisprudence.

In British India, for example, the colonial administration codified Muslim family law through the Shariat Application Act of 1937, which aimed to apply Islamic law to Muslims in matters of personal status while leaving other aspects of law under the colonial legal system. This codification process often involved selective interpretations of Islamic texts, leading to a rigid and sometimes narrow application of family law. Similarly, in French-controlled North Africa, Muslim family law was marginalized in favor of French civil law, though it continued to be applied in certain personal matters.

Post-Colonial Reforms: The Search For Identity And Modernity

The post-colonial period saw a resurgence of interest in Muslim family law as newly independent Muslim-majority countries sought to assert their identity and sovereignty. Legislative reforms during this period were often motivated by the desire to modernize family law while remaining faithful to Islamic principles. This period also saw significant variation in how different countries approached the reform of Muslim family laws.

In Egypt, the 1920s and 1930s witnessed significant reforms in family law, particularly in the areas of divorce and polygamy. These reforms were driven by a combination of feminist activism, legal scholarship, and state intervention. The Egyptian government sought to balance the demands of modernity with Islamic tradition by introducing reforms that limited the grounds for divorce, restricted polygamy, and enhanced the legal status of women. Similar reforms were enacted in other Arab countries, including

Tunisia and Morocco, where the post-colonial state played a central role in shaping family law.

In South Asia, the post-colonial period saw diverse approaches to Muslim family law. Pakistan, for instance, implemented significant reforms in the 1960s under the leadership of General Ayub Khan. The Muslim Family Laws Ordinance of 1961 introduced a range of progressive measures, including the requirement for judicial approval of polygamy, restrictions on unilateral divorce by men (talaq), and enhanced rights for women in matters of inheritance and child custody. These reforms were met with both support and resistance, reflecting the complex interplay between tradition and modernity in Muslim societies.

The Role Of Islamic Revivalism And Political Islam

The late 20th century witnessed the rise of Islamic revivalism and political Islam, movements that had a profound impact on Muslim family law. In many countries, the push for legislative reforms was influenced by these movements, which often sought to reassert the primacy of Islamic law in public life. This period also saw the emergence of debates over the compatibility of Islamic law with human rights, particularly in relation to women's rights.

In Iran, the 1979 Islamic Revolution led to the establishment of a theocratic regime that sought to implement Islamic law across all aspects of life, including family law. The new regime reversed many of the progressive reforms introduced during the reign of the Shah, reintroducing traditional interpretations of marriage, divorce, and inheritance laws. However, the post-revolutionary period also saw ongoing debates and adjustments within the framework of Islamic law, reflecting the dynamic nature of legal interpretation in Iran.

In contrast, Tunisia pursued a different path. Under the leadership of President Habib Bourguiba, Tunisia introduced some of the most progressive family law reforms in the Muslim world. The 1956 Code of Personal Status abolished polygamy, granted women equal rights in divorce, and established judicial oversight of marriage contracts. These reforms were grounded in a modernist interpretation of Islam and were part of a broader effort to secularize Tunisian society. Despite challenges from Islamist movements, Tunisia has largely maintained its progressive stance on family law, particularly after the 2011 revolution.

Globalization And The Influence Of International Human Rights Norms

The late 20th and early 21st centuries have been marked by increasing globalization, which has had a significant impact on Muslim family law. The spread of international human rights norms, particularly those related to gender equality and women's rights, has led to growing pressure on Muslim-majority countries to reform their family laws.

In some cases, international pressure has resulted in significant legislative reforms. Morocco's 2004 reform of its family code, known as the Moudawana, is a prime example. The reform process was influenced by both domestic advocacy groups and international organizations, leading to a new family code that enhanced women's rights in marriage, divorce, and inheritance. The Moudawana has been widely praised as a model for balancing Islamic principles with modern human rights standards.

However, the impact of globalization on Muslim family law has not been uniform. In some countries, the influence of international norms has been resisted or selectively incorporated into domestic legal systems. For instance, in Saudi Arabia, the application of Muslim family law remains closely tied to traditional interpretations of Islamic texts, with limited incorporation of international human rights standards. The recent reforms under Crown Prince Mohammed bin Salman, while significant, have focused more on social and economic issues than on comprehensive changes to family law.

The Role Of Women In Driving Legislative Reform

Women have played a crucial role in driving legislative reform in Muslim family laws. From the early 20th century to the present, women's rights activists, scholars, and legal professionals have advocated for changes to family laws that enhance gender equality and protect women's rights within the framework of Islamic law.

In many countries, women-led movements have successfully pushed for reforms that address issues such as polygamy, divorce, and child custody. For example, in Malaysia, women's groups have been at the forefront of efforts to reform the country's Islamic family laws, advocating for changes that address gender-based discrimination and improve the legal status of women. These efforts have led to incremental reforms, though challenges remain in achieving full gender equality in family law.

In other contexts, women have also played a role in resisting regressive changes to family law. In Algeria, for instance, women activists have mobilized against attempts to roll back the progressive reforms introduced after independence. Their activism has been instrumental in maintaining the gains made in women's rights and family law.

Contemporary Debates And Challenges

Today, the reform of Muslim family laws remains a contentious and evolving issue. Contemporary debates often center on the tension between tradition and modernity, as well as the challenge of harmonizing Islamic principles with international human rights standards. These debates are particularly acute in areas such as polygamy, inheritance, and the legal status of women in marriage and divorce.

One of the key challenges in contemporary reform efforts is the diversity of interpretations within Islamic jurisprudence. The existence of multiple schools of thought, each with its own interpretations of key issues, complicates the process of legal reform. Additionally, the influence of political and social factors, such as the rise of conservative religious movements, often shapes the direction and scope of reforms.

Another challenge is the role of the state in regulating family law. In some countries, the state has played a proactive role in reforming family laws, often in response to social demands and international pressures. In others, the state has been more reluctant to intervene, leaving family law largely in the hands of religious authorities. This divergence in state involvement has led to significant variation in the application of Muslim family law across the Muslim world.

The global and historical exploration of legislative reform in Muslim family laws reveals a complex and dynamic process influenced by a wide range of factors, including colonialism, modernization, political Islam, globalization, and women's activism. While significant progress has been made in reforming Muslim family laws to reflect the changing needs of society, challenges remain in achieving a balance between tradition and modernity, as well as in reconciling Islamic principles with international human rights standards.

As the world continues to change, the evolution of Muslim family laws will likely continue, shaped by the ongoing interplay between religious, social, and political forces. The future of these laws will depend on the ability of Muslim-majority countries to navigate these complexities while remaining true to the core values of justice and equality that underpin Islamic jurisprudence.

CHAPTER IV

Islamic Law Reforms Through Maqasid-ul-Sharia

Maqasid-ul-Sharia, (objectives of Shariah) is an emerging trend in Islamic legal epistemology. The Islamic Fiqh (jurisprudence), lost its vitality towards the end of the fifteenth century as original thoughts were frowned upon and instead dogmatic imitation (Taqleed) was pursued by Muslim scholars. The new social realities of national states and decolonization of Muslim lands have accelerated new approaches to Fiqh, in order to timely reform Islamic law. New interpretations of Islamic legal cannons are premised upon Maqasid-ul-Sharia.

Maqasid al-Shari'ah may be stated simply as the higher objectives of the rules of the Shari'ah, the observance of which, facilitates the normal functioning of society by enhancing the public good (Maslaha), this implies avoiding actions likely to harm individuals and society. The intent, objective and purpose are simply to achieve social and economic justice as well as enhancing the welfare of the community. According to Ibn Ashur, maqasid al-Shariah (objectives of Shariah) is a term that refers to the preservation of order, achievement of benefit and prevention of harm or corruption, establishment of equality among people, causing the law to be revered, obeyed and effective as well as enabling the Ummah to become powerful, respected and confident.

Protection of Six fundamental rights is at the core of Maqasid-ul-Sharia, viz. life, property, intellect religion and progeny. This modern interpretation is an expanded version of Istihsan (juristic discretion), one of the pillars of *Usul-ul-Fiqh* (Principles of Islamic jurisprudence). Classical scholars like Imam Ghazali, Shatibi, Juvaini and Shah Waliullah

Dehlavi have mentioned this liberal tool of religious interpretation while dealing with ecclesiastical issues.

Maqasid-Ul-Sharia In Classical Religious Cannons

Various Hadeeth from six canonical Hadeeth scriptures point to the Maqasid-ul-Sharia. Hazrat Umar had extensively modified religious rulings on various issues based upon Maqasid-ul-Sharia. In his Hujjathullahil Baligha, Shah Waliullah explains this tenet thus: 'Islam gives much leeway for fluidity and elasticity of laws according to local, cultural, social conditions'.

Quran and Hadeeth emphasize human intellectual faculty to solve legal issues. The diversity of opinions in Islamic legal schools should be read in this context. The scholars of Usul-ul-Fiqh have pointed out to the crucial salience of spatial and temporal contexts while framing Islamic laws. The prominence given to Urf (local customs) highlights this point.

In a nutshell, except a few laws categorically mentioned in Quran and Hadeeth, Maqasid-ul-Sharia could be invoked to explore it more. Diverse opinions of legal scholars on single issues are attributed to the application of Maqasid-ul-Sharia while dealing with legal problems. For example, the divergence of opinion about the nature of witness to a contract in Islamic law is because of the fact that scholars considered local customs and conditions whole pronouncing fatwa.

The changes and modification brought by Hazarat Umar is a befitting example to prove the legal sanction of Maqasid-ul-Sharia in Islamic legal traditions. He applied Ijtihad (independent reasoning) to formulate laws for issues at hand.

Some examples for Maqasid-ul-Sharia from the legal rulings of Hazrat Umar:

1. Compulsory acquisitions of war booty during his reign which was not the standard practice during the Prophet's time.

2. Banning naval battle considering its commensurate risks

3. Changes in the system of Zakat distribution to new converts when people began accepting faith to get Zakat

4. Temporarily suspended chopping of hand of the thieves during the times of drought

Minority Fiqh And New Interpretations

The majority of Islamic laws were codified and institutionalized under the political conditions where Muslims basked in political hegemony. But the migration of Muslims to Europe or the loosing of political patronage in countries like India justified rethinking of Islamic laws to suit the swift churnings in the society. Fiqh al-Aqalliyyat (the jurisprudence of Muslim minorities) is a legal doctrine introduced in the 1990s by Taha Jabir Al-Alwani and Yusuf Al-Qaradawi which asserts that Muslim minorities, especially those residing in the West, deserve a special new legal discipline to address their unique religious needs that differ from those of Muslims residing in Islamic countries. Developed as a means of assisting Muslim minorities in the West, it deals with problems Muslims face in countries where they are minorities and focuses more on devising exceptional rulings pertaining to their unique circumstances.

So the classical opinions of barring Muslims living in countries with a majority non-Muslim population and enjoining to migrate from such places are rejected by new approach to a political understanding of Islam. Maqasid-ul-Sharia is a vital tool in evolving minority fiqh as it accommodates changing realities of political developments. The futile clinging to old classical laws is fraught with challenges and militates against the canonical exhortations in this regard.

Rethinking Of Fiqh In The Indian Context Based On Maqasid-Ul-Sharia

India has rich copious traditions of original additions to Fiqh knowledge; but it lost, as a general decadence set in among the faithful and gradually Islam became educationally morbid and culturally dogmatic. Revival of Islamic law based on Maqasid-ul-Sharia is too important in the contemporary Indian context that no sane scholar can object to this. New trends of Islamic epistemology could be used to reinvigorate the soul of

Islam.

Issues like electoral politics, women participation, upward social mobility and new economic realities are to be reframed on the solid basis of Maqasid-ul-Sharia. Islam is never a barren land of imitation but fertile space for suitable evolution. Various pressing issues of Muslim community in India could be amicably solved by using the liberal tools of Maqasid-ul-Sharia.

CHAPTER V

Islamic Jurisprudence: Lost Dialogue And Creativity

The inclination to engage in debate and discourse is deeply ingrained in human nature, a principle underscored in the Qur'an itself with the proclamation that "Man is a great reasoner" (Surat al-Kahf). This innate tendency toward argumentation enables individuals to develop nuanced perspectives on various issues, allowing for a thorough examination of right and wrong. In the realm of Islamic scholarship, this propensity for debate is evident in the writings of traditional ulama, where authors often assume the roles of both plaintiff and defendant, engaging in self-reflective dialogue to refine their viewpoints. This intellectual exchange is integral to Islamic jurisprudence (Fiqh), a field characterized by its vastness and adaptability to diverse contexts over time. The enduring relevance of ancient legal texts in contemporary society is highlighted by legal scholars like Mahmood Kooria, who draw parallels between Islamic jurisprudence and concepts such as the Butterfly Effect and Longue Duree, demonstrating how small actions or movements in the past can lead to significant consequences in the present. Moreover, the interpretability of Fiqh allows for continual reinterpretation and adaptation, ensuring its applicability to evolving societal norms and challenges.

The dynamic nature of Islamic jurisprudence is exemplified in the interpretation and commentary of seminal texts like Imam Nawawi's Minhaj, which has undergone multiple reinterpretations across different regions and time periods. These commentaries serve to contextualize the original texts and express dissenting opinions, often adopting the role of the logician in scrutinizing and analyzing the arguments presented. The tradition of scholarly debate within Islamic jurisprudence has been subject to criticism, with some scholars questioning the productivity and originality of commentaries. However, scholars like Ahmed El Shamsy have defended the value of these commentaries, emphasizing their critical analysis and contribution to the development of Islamic legal thought.

Islamic jurisprudence is characterized by diversity and dissent, with scholars recognizing the importance of understanding different interpretations to grasp the full scope of Fiqh. The process of dissent is approached with precision and respect for evidence, as exemplified by instances of disagreement between scholars recorded in autobiographical accounts and scholarly works. These debates serve to broaden perspectives and sharpen critical thinking skills, fostering greater affinity and understanding among different schools of thought within Islamic jurisprudence.

In the pursuit of truth and understanding, debates within Islamic jurisprudence are guided by moral values and principles of respectful discourse. Scholars emphasize the importance of humility, patience, and moral integrity in engaging in debates, highlighting Islam's emphasis on ethical conduct in intellectual exchange. The systematic study of debate within Islamic jurisprudence has revealed its evolution over time, with scholars like Imam Khaffal Ashashi pioneering the use of technical terminology to outline the process of debate. The history of debate within Islamic jurisprudence is divided into distinct phases, each marked by significant developments and shifts in approach.

Contemporary scholarship continues to explore the modes and conditions of debate within Islamic jurisprudence, with scholars examining the legacy of historical figures like Imam Shirazi and the impact of their debates on the evolution of Islamic law. The interdisciplinary nature of this research, drawing on fields such as history, philosophy, and law, underscores the complexity and richness of Islamic intellectual tradition. By engaging in open dialogues and scholarly debates, scholars, religious leaders, and community members can critically examine traditional interpretations of Islamic law and work towards meaningful reforms that uphold the core principles of justice, equality, and compassion.

Debate And The Evolution Of Islamic Law: Seeking Harmony Between Tradition And Progress

Islamic law, like many legal systems, faces the challenge of balancing its rich history and core principles with the evolving needs of contemporary society. Debate and discussion have long played a vital role in navigating this dynamic, allowing scholars and communities to explore diverse interpretations and consider fresh perspectives. The Qur'an itself encourages intellectual discourse, and proponents of debate argue that engaging in open exchange is crucial for reexamining traditional interpretations in light of modern contexts. Issues like gender equality, human rights, and social justice call for careful adaptation of jurisprudence while staying true to core Islamic values.

Figures like Imam Shirazi exemplify the historical value of scholarly debate. His prowess in debate and willingness to engage with other schools of thought fostered mutual understanding and broadened perspectives. However, caution is necessary. Islamic law's complexity calls for a nuanced approach that considers historical context, diverse interpretations, and potential social and religious implications. Imposing reforms solely through debate is unlikely to achieve lasting change. Instead, respectful dialogue, inclusivity, and a sensitive understanding of diverse perspectives are essential. Organic shifts in interpretation and societal change often contribute more to meaningful reform than purely formal pronouncements or debates.

In conclusion, debates within Islamic jurisprudence play a vital role in shaping the interpretation and application of Islamic law, fostering intellectual exchange and mutual understanding among diverse Muslim communities. By embracing inclusivity, diversity of perspectives, and ethical conduct in discourse, scholars and community members can navigate complex issues and work towards reform that resonates with the needs and aspirations of contemporary society. While debates offer a platform for exploring different viewpoints, true reform arises through organic shifts in interpretation and societal changes, requiring sensitivity, caution, and respect for diverse perspectives. Through thoughtful engagement and dialogue, Islamic jurisprudence can continue to evolve and adapt to meet the challenges of the modern world while remaining rooted in the fundamental values of Islam.

CHAPTER VI

Feminizing Islam: Global Responses

Attitudes towards women within the Muslim world have become the greatest example of the grave degradation that has taken place in the Muslim community. The Muslim woman and her headscarf are being discussed again in the world through the women of Iran. Its ripples are rising in India too. It has been a long time since the conservative clergy and their minions started throwing 'fatwa baits' at her, but now that the girls have gained the insight to recognize such baits, the religious authorities who claim to have the right to subvert the Muslims are in a state of complete disarray. There is no point in blaspheming against these people who do not turn their attention to the words they utter, even if they reach the result of lying down and spitting. However, the bright chapters of the past need to be placed against the background of the current female awakenings in the Muslim world. It would be an injustice to those individuals and to history not to dwell on some of those struggles that are not so far behind.

In the second half of the 19th century and the beginning of the 20th century, Muslim women opened the front of struggle in different countries. Religious leaders and political power centres joined hands to liberate the victimized women and girls from the society of that time. Some women fought along the lines of women's liberation in the West, while others saw liberation from within their own existence. Accordingly, they forcefully and persistently questioned the male narratives of Islamic precepts through historical re-reading and logic. They found gender equality, equality and justice, which they interpret as modern values, from these same creeds. At the same time, 'Islam', which deviated from these same values, was constantly ridiculed and scorned by the world.

Peace was alien to these fighters in the ways of justice and rights that Islam had opened before them. Because of the internal and external agitations, rejections, jails and beatings were sought. But the reality is that the governments of many countries had to kneel before them in the last century. Laws were rewritten to accommodate women in education, suffrage, family and social positions. They have made unprecedented progress in many areas.

All of them were qualified and capable enough to compete with or stand ahead of the male world of that time in terms of spiritual and material education. Had they been able to continue to develop the way of their investigations and struggles, it would have been possible to transform and introduce Islam to the level of the liberating vision of modern societies instead of being labelled as a '6th century tribal religion'! However, later, attempts were made to make these women's struggles invisible in the dustbin of history by the authoritarian rule in Muslim countries.

In the second half of the 20th century, there was another reason for the decline of those advances. One of them is the West's 'war on terror'. When the neo-colonial invasions that started from Iraq and spread all over the West Asia destroyed the Muslim countries, the women's lives in those countries were also fragmented. The combination of war and flight made it hellish. On one side, the black hands of the priesthood, on the other, the imperialist foreigners who pretended to be the saviors of Muslim countries. Between the devil and the sea, the female awakenings that had occurred earlier in the Muslim world had weakened roots.

Islam has been relegated to the past by those who have no capacity to guide the Muslims of the modern age, either spiritually or intellectually. Theirs was an approach and intervention that poured oil into the post-September 11 state of affairs in the Muslim world. The attempt was to defend all external attacks on it as a religious community by cloaking it in strict orthodoxy. The body of a Muslim woman was a rusted sheet of it. They have convinced the world within their sphere of influence that its internal and external challenges can only be covered up. Male and female slaves were created accordingly. Arab nationalism was co-opted to label neo-conservatism as Islam. Modern technology has also been used to spread misinterpreted creeds around the world. The result was that misogyny, a vestige of pre-Islamic Arabian tribal life, was exported to various parts in the name of Islam. Its apparent spread was through the black long dress.

The propagandists of neo-liberalism along with the Muslim man come in as the real beneficiaries of the obfuscation of this past in the new circumstances where all democratic interventions towards the problems of the Muslim woman are overturned and hidden on a piece of cloth. Muslim women have begun to rise up in many countries with the support of the new social media while this invasion is intensifying by suppressing the local diversity and rights struggles of Islam. It was a succession of early and later interrupted awakenings. That is what is unfolding in Iran now. Its waves spread to many lands.

While the Muslim community around the world is going through turbulent times under the sharp claws of imperialism and fascism, the power priesthood is busy blocking the outside light and wind with the easily acceptable shield of 'Islamic doctrine', attacking the faith and confidence of women. Unfortunately, in Kerala, which boasts of being a very fertile ground for Muslim 'renaissance', such reform efforts can be seen being trampled with utter disdain. Its stench is emitted by the words of the Maulavis.

At various points in modern Islamic history there have been brilliant women who have recognized the dangerous depth of this systematic anti-feminist construction and re-read it. The first wave of it was the Egyptian women's rights struggles of the last century. Through this, famous fighters who were not brought close to reading areas, including those of India, are being introduced. In the language of the mullahs here, the 'libertines' who challenged the religion.

Huda Sharavi: The Woman Who Pulled Off Her Headscarf In The Face Of The Priesthood

Huda Shaarawi was born in 1879 to Egypt's extreme orthodoxy. Huda Sharawi is the first name on the list of women who changed Egypt. She is also considered to be the pioneer of the women's movement in that country. She was born into the 'harem' system where men and women were separated. Her father was Muhammad Sultan Pasha, who was active in Egyptian national politics.

Despite being born into an elite family, they too were destined to grow up in oblivion. In those days girls were denied schooling. Women huddled indoors in secluded rooms and wore face veils when going out. Huda Sharawi's situation was no different. She was deeply disappointed that she was denied the same schooling as her brother. She was deeply saddened by the family's neglect of her studies and their secondary attitude towards her as a girl. Huda realized that being a woman stood between her and her freedom.

The Egyptian Feminist Union was founded in 1923 by Huda Shaarawi, president of the Women's Central Committee of the national political party 'Wafd' in 1920. In March of the same year, she removed her headscarf and face covering from a train at the Cairo railway station. He jumped out of the train with his head open. Other women were invited to join this movement

At the age of 13, she was forced to marry her cousin, Ali Shaarawi, who was 40 years older than her. She had no choice but to give in to save her family's honor. But Huda decided to speak out about his pain and start the revolution himself. So as a child she started speaking to people against this injustice. As a result, many women came out of hiding for the first time in their lives. In 1908, under the leadership of Huda, the first secular charity organization run by Egyptian women was formed. It was for service activities for underprivileged women and children.

Huda and her husband Ali were strong supporters of Egyptian independence from Great Britain. In 1920, Huda became the president of the Women's Central Committee of a national political party called 'WAFD'. The open participation of women in the national movement marked a turning point in Egyptian society.

Never before had so many women been openly involved in political activities. After her husband's death, Huda Sherawi shifted her focus from the nationalist movement to efforts towards women's equality. In 1923, she founded the Egyptian Feminist Union. It spurred women's suffrage, personal law reforms, and educational opportunities for girls and women.

In March of the same year, an incident that shook the country took place. It was when Huda Shaarawi was returning home after attending the International Women's Conference in Rome. She removed her headscarf with face covering from the train at the Cairo railway station. He jumped out of the train with his head open. Other women were invited to join this movement. This was the first anti-headscarf protest in Egypt. It became a strong blow on the face of the religious priesthood. Many women came out from inside as part of the protest. Huda then ventured into the practical ways of women's education. Schools were started for girls. An organization called the Egyptian Feminist Union was also formed. Their fight to raise the marriageable age of girls to 16 was successful. Huda Shaarawi remained president of the Egyptian Feminist Union for the rest of her life and became the founding president of the Arab Feminist Union in 1945. She left this world in 1947 after constant struggle for the liberation and rights of women and children.

Doria Shafiq: The Daughter Of The Storm-Turned-Nile

Doria Shefiq, a poet and editor, was one of the prominent leaders of the women's liberation movement in Egypt in the mid-1940s. As a result of their struggle, Egyptian women won the right to vote.

Doria was one of the first Egyptian girls to graduate from secondary school with a baccalaureate degree at the age of 18. The Egyptian Ministry of Education awarded her a scholarship to study at the Sorbonne University in Paris. He received his PhD in Philosophy. She wrote a thesis on equal rights for women. When she returned to Egypt from France in 1940 after her studies, she wanted to contribute to the education of her country's youth through teaching, but was denied a teaching position by the Dean of the Faculty of Literature at Cairo University on the grounds of being 'liberal'.

The event that caused a storm in the Egyptian Parliament took place in February 1951. Doria Shefiq secretly brought 1500 women to the parliament through Bint Al Nil and the Egyptian Feminist Union. She stalled Parliament for hours with several demands related to women's socio-economic rights. This created a huge uproar in the country

He then became the editor-in-chief of La Femme Nouvelle, a French cultural and literary magazine. It was decided to publish an Arabic magazine called Bint Al Nil (Daughter of the Nile) aimed at educating Egyptian women and helping them play the most effective role in the family and society. The first edition sold out immediately after its release in November 1945.

Two years later Doria formed the 'Bint Al Nil' Union to address the primary social issues of women and ensure their inclusion in the country's policies. Efforts were made to eradicate illiteracy by setting up centres for the purpose across the country and setting up employment offices and cafeterias for employed women.

The event that caused a storm in the Egyptian Parliament took place in February 1951. Through Bint Al Nil and the Egyptian Feminist Union, Doria secretly brought 1500 women to the parliament. She stalled Parliament for hours with several demands related to women's socio-economic rights. This created a huge uproar in the country. In the same year, Doria formed a uniformed paramilitary unit. She led a senior brigade to surround and shut down a bank in the country. Police arrested them during the demonstration.

After the Egyptian revolution of 1952, the government invited Bint al-Nil to recognize it as a political party. Doria Shafiq herself became its president. In March 1954, she went on an eight-day hunger strike in protest against the formation of the Constitution Committee without women. They ended their strike after receiving written assurances from President Najib that he would commit to a constitution that respects women's rights. As a result of the interest sparked by the hunger strike, Doria was invited to lecture on Egyptian women in Asia, Europe and America. She travelled to Italy, England, France, the United States, Japan, India, Sri Lanka and Pakistan. As a result of Doria's tireless efforts, women got the right to vote under the 1956 Constitution.

Doria went on a second hunger strike at the Indian Embassy to protest the dictatorial rule of President Jamal Abdul Nasser. Nasser put them under house arrest. Their names were banned from the newspapers and their magazines from circulation. They waged an unrelenting and continuous struggle against the priesthood and the state. In addition to print media, she has written a novel, 'El Eslave de Sultan' (The King's Slave) and several poems about the slavery of women to men.

Nawal El Saadawi: Owner of Bright Liberation Politics

It seems that there is no other women's liberator in the world who has fought and struggled with the authoritarian system within religion and within capitalism like Nawal El Saadawi. Nawal Saadawi is the second wave in the fight for women's rights in Egypt. That life was a vast sea of experiences that at once baffled and thrilled those who sought to know them. A brilliant personality who shined in diverse fields like writer, activist, physician, mental health expert, teacher and organizer.

Till she left this world on March 21, 2021, at the age of 89, she continued to radiate the fresh energy of unique thought and bravery. For decades, she has shared her story and perspectives with the world through novels, essays, autobiographies, and lively conversations. Their brutal honesty and unwavering dedication to advancing women's political and sexual rights struck a chord enough to inspire generations. Nawal El Saadawi made the most accurate political observation that 'oppression of women has its roots in the global capitalist system, supported by religious fundamentalism'.

Saadawi's works have been translated from Arabic into more than thirty languages. She was a strong critic of capitalism as well as religions. She made the most accurate political observation that 'the oppression of women is rooted in the global capitalist system, supported by religious fundamentalism'.

Born the second of nine children in a village on the outskirts of Cairo in 1931, Saadawi's life was surprisingly eventful. Saadawi's father was an official in the Egyptian Ministry of Education. During the Egyptian Revolution of 1919, he was exiled to a small town on the banks of the Nile as a result of campaigning against British occupation. Being relatively progressive, he taught his daughter to grow up with self-respect. Those parents encouraged their children's education. Even so, Saadawi was subjected to female genital mutilation (FGM) at the age of six according to the local custom. In her book 'The Hidden Face of Eve', she describes the painful brutality on the bathroom floor. She campaigned against this practice throughout her life. It was argued that it was meant to oppress women. Egypt banned FGM in 2008. Yet Saadawi continued to fight against it.

There was an attempt to get her married at the age of 10, but her mother objected. Sadavi learned at an early age that daughters are valued less than sons in that society. When her grandmother once said, 'A boy is worth at least 15 girls,' she cried out against it. Saadawi wrote his first novel at the age of 13! The early demise of her parents put the burden of taking care of the large family on her shoulders, but she did not get discouraged. He graduated in medicine from Cairo University in 1955, worked as a doctor, including in villages, and eventually specialized in psychiatry. He joined the Egyptian government as director of public health.

Ever since she dared to speak out dangerously, Saadawi has faced death threats and imprisonment. They never retreated in fear. 'I am telling the truth. "Truth is cruel and dangerous," they once said. A friend called her 'born with a fighting spirit'. About Omnia Amin Saadawi. She got a fighting spirit and self-esteem from her father. She proudly described herself as a dark-skinned Egyptian woman from a young age. Fearlessly looking the priesthood and its political forms in the face, they exposed the truth. At one point, Egyptian President Anwar Sadat put them behind bars.

In 1972, while director of public health, she was fired after publishing a non-fiction book, Women and Sex, which criticized FGM and the sexual harassment of women. The magazine 'Health' founded by Saadawi was closed down. Yet speaking and writing did not stop. In 1975, the novel 'Woman at Point Zero' was published. The novel was based on the real-life account of a woman on death row.

In 1977, she wrote 'Hidden Face of Eve', which chronicled her experiences as a village doctor witnessing sexual harassment, murders and prostitution. This created a great stir. Critics have accused it of subverting the role models of Arab women. In September 1981, under the regime of President Anwar Sadat, Saadawi was arrested and imprisoned for several months. She scribbled notes on dirty toilet paper using an eyebrow pencil from her sex worker in prison.

After Anwar Sadat's assassination, Saadawi was released from prison. But their work was censored and their books banned. In the years that followed, death threats came from fundamentalists. The courts went up. Eventually he became an expatriate in the US. She has accepted offers to teach in the Department of Asian and African Languages at Duke University in North Carolina and at the University of Washington. From there the attacks on religion, colonialism and Western hypocrisy continued.

He later held positions at several prestigious colleges and universities, including Cairo University, Harvard, Yale, Columbia, Sorbonne, Georgetown, Florida State University, University of California, and Berkeley. She received honorary degrees from three continents. But their only dream or hope was recognition from Egypt. She said that she has received honours all over the world but none from her own country. Saadawi returned to his beloved Egypt in 1996. In the 2004 election, he tried to run for the presidency. In 2011, he was in Cairo's Tahrir Square to protest against President Hosni Mubarak. He spent his last years in Cairo with his son and daughter.

Leila Ahmed: Enemy Of Arab Nationalism

Later, there were attempts to interpret from the foundations of the religion that much of the emancipation of women was embedded in the history, ideas, and practices of Islam itself, rejecting the ideas of Western feminism that were tied only to upper-class women's rights consciousness. The most notable in this stream was Dr. Laila Ahmed. She was a professor at Ansar University in Cairo. Leila Ahmed's interventions were not like those of her predecessors Huda Shaarawi, Doria Shefiq or Nawal Saadawl.

They made attempts to interpret feminism in Islam on the basis of the Qur'an. In her 1992 book 'Women and Gender in Islam', she argued that it was the patriarchal interpretations of Islam that pushed women to such a subordinate position. Islam came into the hands of the Mullahs and their rule came over the religion. Leila observes that if it had remained in the hands of the Maulvis, the possibilities would have been very transformative in the Islamic world.

Leila Ahmed said that Islam will automatically develop and evolve only if it becomes a jurisprudence that is both spiritually and morally appropriate for human society.

Much before the modern world, Islam gave women a place in the mainstream in marriage, divorce, family life, business and other socio-political spheres like property rights. However, she emphatically stated that the real women's emancipatory potential within Islam was being undermined where the existing conservative clergy and administrations were not ready to interpret it in a modern way.

Leila took a strong stance against Egyptian Arab nationalism. They argued that Arab nationalism was a form of cultural imperialism. They warned that it would erode not only the Arabic-speaking population but also the cultural diversity and diversity of non-Muslims. Leila Ahmed said that Islam will automatically develop and evolve only if it becomes a jurisprudence that is both spiritual and moral. From Egypt's cultural diversity, she wrote 'A Border Passage' in 1999, which is very relevant in the new global political situation.

Fatima Mernissi: The Dangerous Muslim Scholar

Beyond the two absolute concepts of men and women, the regress made by a faithful Muslim woman to history by removing the hundreds of vestiges of the priesthood, which later came as a subversion on the content of gender equality and justice in Islam, is surprising. When Fatima Mernissi, a Moroccan woman, travelled through those paths that were not followed by many, some harsh truths that had not been revealed to the world until then were revealed. Mernice wrote that he knew that traveling back in time would be dangerous.

Mernissi made the crucial findings that the hijab in Islam is not a woman's head covering, but rather the idea of separating the inner world of the home from the outer public space in the Qur'an. The Qur'anic word on hijab, which was revealed to teach the Arab people proper manners at that time, was later subjected to a massive subversion and turned into a piece of cloth covering a woman.

She was not denying the misogynistic hadiths (prophetic teachings) currently celebrated in the Muslim world by turning a blind eye to being a woman by its very nature. Rather, it led a careful investigation into the origin of alleged misogyny attributed to the Prophet Muhammad. Mernissi's writings, which are based on the knowledge that is the foundation of patriarchy, are too dangerous for the Muslim male supremacists who celebrate Islam as their own 'religion'.

Examining the linguistic, social, and historical aspects of the hijab, Mernissi explores the linguistic, social, and historical aspects of the hijab, revealing that the veil that came down from 'heaven' was used to cover women, separate them from men, and separate them from God.

They made the crucial findings that the hijab in Islam is not a woman's head covering, but rather the idea of separating the inner world of the home from the outer public space that the Qur'an proposed. The Qur'anic word of hijab, which was revealed to teach the Arab people of that time proper manners, was later subjected to a massive subversion and turned into a piece of cloth to cover a woman.

Prophet Muhammad's residence was always accessible to his followers at any time. Moreover, there was no division between his private and public life. The said word of God was born when the people visited him without any formality. The verse teaching that you should not enter his house without permission later evolved into a division based on gender. Examining the linguistic, social, and historical aspects of the hijab, Mernissi reveals that the veil that came down from 'heaven' was used to cover women, separate them from men, and separate them from God.

Another serious fact is that they discovered that the internal disintegration of the Muslim world took place immediately after the death of the Prophet Muhammad, after a careful and long search into the hidden paths of history. The unusual and surprising investigations and readings by a Muslim scholar were, however, ignored in the Arab masculinity milieu.

According to Mernissi, the famous hadith compiler al-Bukhari found that 5,96,725 fake hadiths were in circulation two centuries after the death of the Prophet Muhammad. Some spread false sayings which they claimed to be from the Prophet for their gain. They were twisting the contents of the hadith and making changes in the series of persons who transmitted it!

The Muslim man argues that any Muslim woman who stands for dignity and citizenship rights is out of place in this society. They are easily accused of being brainwashed by the West because they do not understand their own religious tradition and cultural identity. Mernissi unequivocally reminds us that our quest for pride, democracy, human rights and equal participation in the political and social affairs of our country originates from authentic Muslim traditions and not from imported Western values, and therefore, this knowledge empowers us as Muslim women to walk proudly before the world.

Mernissi's authoritative finding was that hundreds of years before the Prophet was alive, lively debates about women's emancipation and various approaches to it were being discussed in the streets of Medina, through which women had grasped multifaceted rights. Mernice's was a leap into the truths that our history has deliberately hidden about these women.

"Thousands of women flocked to the Prophet's city of Medina in the seventh century from the aristocratic patriarchate of Mecca because Islam promised dignity and equality to men and women, master and servant alike." Many young tribal women and slaves alike were attracted to the new religion. The prophet of this religion spoke out for human dignity and equal rights while raising serious challenges to the establishment and became a nightmare for the authorities in Mecca. But Mernice says the greatest conundrum of our time is that his message of universal equality is viewed as an import from the outside world.

Those who argue that gender equality is a foreign matter should be aware of the stark reality that the narrow streets of Medina were already riddled with gender equality disputes 15 centuries ago. She points out in her book 'Weil and the Male Elite' that while it took the West many centuries to digest the ideas of democracy and gender equality, Muslims had to respond within a few decades of the establishment of Islam.

Mernici's 'Beyond the Veil', published in 1975, has become the most widely read classic in English. Through this book, she examines the Arab world and Muslim women's lives from the levels of anthropology and sociology.

Amina Wadood: A Woman Who Challenged By Deeds

Amina Wadud was the Mary Tesla of an Afro-American family until she recognized and embraced the liberating possibilities within Islam through research and study. In 1994, she delivered a Jummah (Friday prayer) sermon at a mosque in Cape Town, South Africa, unlike other prominent female figures in the Muslim world. It was read as a powerful blow to the head of the priestly aristocracy. Ten years after that happened, in 2005, she led Friday prayer itself.

Both men and women rallied behind the woman without distinction. With this, they have become extremely dangerous women who should not be approached in the traditional Muslim world including Kerala. However, regardless of such insults and threats, today he is busy spreading his research and readings in different parts of the world like the US, South Asia, Africa and Europe.

Amina Wadood joined Virginia Commonwealth University as a professor in the Department of Religion and Philosophy in 1999 and retired from there in 2008. The book 'Qur'an and Women' is enough to understand the depth of their knowledge and inquisitiveness.

Asma Barlas: The Spark of Feminist Readings of Islam

Another woman at the forefront of feminist readings of Islam is Professor Asma Barlas, author of 'Believing Women in Islam', which examines patriarchal interpretations of the Qur'an historically. Asma, a Pakistani-American writer and academic, has an independent and strong personality. Asma Barlas has stated that she rejects 'Islamic feminism' unless it can be defined as a discourse of gender equality and social justice.

Born in Lahore, Pakistan in 1950, her education extended to the US. Asma Barlas deconstructs the notions of women and gender entirely from within the Qur'an and not through Muslim cultural practices or Western media stereotypes. The book 'Believing Women in Islam: Unreading Patriarchal Interpretations of the Qur'an is a great contribution to those who want to study Islam in that sense.

Their writings pose a serious challenge to the ego of the religious authorities and the conventional Muslim world, who seek justification from the Qur'an for sexual oppression, inequality, and patriarchy. Asma Barlas has stated that she rejects 'Islamic feminism' unless it can be defined as a discourse of gender equality and social justice. Through their studies, they found that the

Qur'an enjoins justice for all human beings across the public-private continuum over their existence.

Asma, who holds an MA in English Literature and Philosophy, an MA in Journalism from Punjab University and a PhD in International Studies from the University of Denver, was one of the first Pakistani women to enter the Foreign Service in 1976. After six years they were disbanded on the orders of General Ziaul Haq. In 1991, he joined the Department of Political Studies at Ithaca College. For 12 years she was the founding director of the Centre for the Study of Culture, Race, and Ethnicity. In 2008, he also served in the Department of Philosophy at the University of Amsterdam.

So many brilliant women in the modern world have breathed life into the rebirth of the dead research of ijtihad, which has led the Muslim world to decline in every sense. There is no doubt that if the world of deep investigations and ideas raised by such personalities is opened up through debates, then this nation will escape from the current poverty of thought and uncertainty.

Indian Muslim women can learn a great deal from Muslim women reformers like Begum Rokeya Sakhawat Hossain and Asma Jahangir. Firstly, they can draw inspiration from their courage and determination in challenging societal norms and advocating for women's rights. These reformers demonstrated that change is possible through education, activism, and a steadfast commitment to justice.

From Begum Rokeya, Indian Muslim women can learn the importance of education as a tool for empowerment. Rokeya's establishment of schools for Muslim girls emphasized the transformative power of education in breaking down barriers and enabling women to assert their rights and independence. Her message underscores the significance of seeking knowledge and self-improvement as pathways to personal and societal advancement.

Similarly, Asma Jahangir's advocacy for human rights and gender equality provides valuable lessons for Indian Muslim women. Jahangir's fearless pursuit of justice and her unwavering dedication to challenging discrimination serve as a beacon for those fighting against oppression. Her emphasis on the principles of equality and dignity within Islam resonates with Indian Muslim women, encouraging them to assert their rights within the framework of their faith.

Overall, Indian Muslim women can learn from these reformers the importance of resilience, solidarity, and active engagement in efforts to promote gender equality and social justice. They can draw strength from their legacy and work towards creating a more inclusive and equitable society for themselves and future generations.

CHAPTER VII

Sexual Minority Politics: Thoughts On The Muslim Political Position

Muslim minority politics needs to be prepared to go beyond the language of prosecution and confront sexual minority politics. A political solidarity that takes difference seriously needs to develop. The reduction of modernist criticism and criticism of liberalism to superficial moralism helps Islamophobes. Both the sexual minority community and the Muslim minority community in India need to unite in the fight against oppression while maintaining their mutual differences of opinion. I do not think that Muslim politics in India is free from 'homophobia', nor that sexual minority politics is free from 'Islamophobia'. In this regard, some moves by the secular new media are turning into a way to hide Islamophobia under the pretence of opposing homophobia.

We must consider the context of state agendas that criminalize minority individuals and communities. Ways of uniting different social/political groups by setting aside prejudices, through mutual dialogue, and maintaining disagreements and differences are constantly evolving at the national level. Such practical experiences broaden the political experience of various minority communities.

Good Life Or Safe Life?

There are many views among Muslims on what constitutes a good life. Consider the example of a Tablighi Jamaat worker's approach to the good life not being very acceptable to Salafis in India. That is, feminism, not just mainstream LGBTIQ approaches, on the issue of what constitutes a good sex life is multi-faceted. Many reasons to disagree with the likes of secularism – as a majority view – can be found in Islamic thought and Islam gives this space of thought. Muslims believe that alcohol is divinely forbidden as the basis of a good life. But the crucial issue is not that this prohibition does not apply to other individuals or communities on the issue of what to drink. Everyone's right to eat food safely without fear should be protected. In Islamic thought, a secure life is as important as a good life.

LGBTIQ politics on a peaceful life, safe from persecution and exclusion, has to be protected. Disagreements about the good life are not an obstacle to secularism and the like. It goes without saying that religious differences are not an obstacle when it comes to political unity. The right to a secure life is different from the different views that individuals or communities have about the good life.

The common minimum program on this issue is that while disagreeing with mainstream LGBTQ communities about the meaning of sexuality, it is possible for them to live safe and dignified lives just like anyone else.

Sexual Politics And Community: Trial Or Solidarity?

Membership of the nation is something that must be proven by law through years of residence in the country (domicility), birth, and written documents such as your and your parents' birth certificates. That is citizenship. Membership in all nation-states that have adopted liberal democracy as their ideology is something that needs to be proven.

Is membership of the Muslim community such a thing? Faith is the determinant of one's life. Once one declares himself a believer, community membership comes naturally, even if no one else is convinced. Membership in the Muslim community is not the same as citizenship in the nation. It is never a land-based thing. This feature needs to be highlighted. It is necessary to highlight the broad political potential of the term 'Muslim'. Community life has to be understood in terms of 'faith' rather than 'legal' citizenship.

But the limitations that occur when the life of faith is seen as merely legalistic terms are vast. For example, in the case of a sexual act, trial under Islamic law, it is not enough to present four eyewitnesses before the court, there are several steps involved in proving it and making it punishable. Therefore, any discussion of any type of sexual activity by any individual is only valid if there are eyewitnesses. Therefore, prosecution is not the methodology of Muslim politics.

Based on this, a person, or a person's experience, cannot be dismissed on the basis of a mass trial, except on legal terms. It is not possible to accuse a person of any kind of sexual activity without the backing of law. In India, where there are no Islamic courts, the civil/criminal courts have to decide the matter. There is an important problem here. All who call themselves Muslims are Muslims. She also belongs to the Muslim community. Another may argue on the basis of evidence that one does not become a Muslim. But no one has the right to expel another from Islam. There is always room for various interpretations. A community is what a person believes himself to be a member of.

Such differences of approach can be seen a lot in the community. An example is the Muslim party fights in Kerala. When the Solidarity Youth Movement was raising environmental issues in Kerala, a section of Salafis said that "fighting against shirk (in the sense of associating partners with God) is more important than fighting against environmental destruction in society". This argument is that adding partners to God is an issue that should be prioritized over environmental issues that affect everyone regardless of caste, religion and gender. Communal life is possible only by maintaining such interpretive differences.

Sexuality And the Modern Foundations Of Religious Criticism

The Muslim critique of sexual politics needs to be viewed more critically in conjunction with the history of modernity. Moral criticism has historical characteristics. This is essential to understand such a political issue more clearly. Modernist criticism is not simple vigilante moralism.

Sexuality has only been a political identity for about 200 years. It has a deep connection with the modern nation-state. It is with the nation that the individual becomes the object of governance.

That is how politics changes to target a person's life, such as how to register a person's birth, how to educate, what to do, when to retire. In earlier societies, neither religion nor politics were aimed at an individual. Sociologically, in pre-modern societies, the individual was seen as an act, not as a totality as in the modern state. The individual in classical Islamic thought is not the individual who is part of the disciplinary authority of modernity.

As the system of the nation-state became a worldwide phenomenon through European colonization, life and sexuality became the object of politics. Thus, religion is forced to address the individual as a totality. It is argued that Muslim social criticism should not be merely a moral concern with the authority of modernity. 'Moral panic' is a social habit of modernity.

In short, sexuality as an identity has only been understood for two hundred years. Sexual minorities have become a political issue in the world in the last fifty years. Discussion starts in Kerala in nineties. It has only been fifteen years that the Muslim community has been conducting studies and discussions about this. Then naturally there will be ambiguities in this regard. There will be a consensus by interacting with each other.

The Political Priority Of Criticism Of Liberalism

Democracy in India is possible through elections. The people who elect the majority become the government. It is generally believed that democracy is a reflection of the majority will of the people. However, courts are institutions that prevent majoritarianism in a democracy. Courts that withhold the rights of individuals and minorities from majoritarianism are, in a sense, turning democracy into a liberal institution. This is the essence of liberal democracy. Democracy is protected from majoritarianism by the liberal institution of 'judiciary'. This is the essence of liberal democracy. Democracy without institutional liberalism turns into majoritarianism and fascism.

In today's Indian situation, democracy has turned into majoritarianism by subverting liberal institutions, and beyond that, it has become fascism, which is part of extremism. Muslim minorities who depend on the courts against fascism are fighting to protect institutional liberalism and thus democracy. Priorities matter in political struggle. Criticism of such an unrecognized liberalism turns out to be mere idealism that helps the fascists.

Another is cultural liberalism. Cultural liberalism, a part of extreme individualism, is the preserve of an elite few in India. Indians are one of the least individualistic societies in the world. The criticism that cultural liberalism fails to recognize minority issues or majoritarianism is valid. Fascists, on the other hand, are cultural purists who oppose all forms of liberalism. Fascists who attack Muslim minorities on the basis of food, clothing, religion, customs and institutions have the backing of cultural nationalism.

Despite its temporary appeasement, cultural liberalism is an elitism whose only option is to either submit to cultural majoritarianism or end up under the knife of the fascists. It can also be seen that the collapse of cultural liberalism is helping fascists to power in the current situation. It is the moral tragedy of cultural liberalism. The bottom line is that fascism succeeds under the guise of not-so-subtle anti-liberalism. The fact is that in the absence of such recognition, the socio-political problems of fascism are trivialized and the political struggle becomes a mere cultural struggle.

The social rhetoric that goes by the name of anti-liberalism turns out to be mere ideology in today's Indian context which cannot shake the power of the fascists. Fascists have a history of promoting ideological exercises aimed at the socially marginalized. There are many debates in North Indian TV shows. But there are few Maulanas in Kerala who discuss the Islamic dimension of condoms to animal rights. With differences Muslim community should come forward to accept the social life of sexual minorities. While having divergent opinion, it's quite possible to unite for this purpose. Muslims, as a minority community should accept sexual minorities too.

CHAPTER VIII

Hijab: The Peaceful Revolution That Changed The World

A flood of books on Islam is evident after 9/11. In, 'Welcome to the Desert of the Real: Five Essays on September 11', Slavoj Zizek observes that when he suddenly sees copies of the Qur'an in Euro-American airports, he is reminded of the white man's astonishment and curiosity as part of the colonial tradition. There are few books that have deviated from the general flow of books published in the last ten years, in favour of, or against, reforming and condemning Islam. The point is that those who oppose and support Islam through Euro-liberal perspectives, as Zizek observes, do not fundamentally differ in their ways of seeing the Islamic world or in their conceptions. Saba Mahmood and Charles Hiskind have overcome the theoretical and analytical weaknesses of these dual narrative methods. Especially Mahmood's 'Politics of Piety: The Islamic Revival and the Feminist Subject'. Saba Mahmood is instrumental in questioning traditional secular-feminist ways of looking at Muslim women.

Saba Mahmood wrote about Muslim women in Egypt. Of course, hugely liberal Islamic feminist narratives exist about Egypt. Huda Shaarawi to Laila Ahmad are in that tradition. Islam must be freed from the hands of practising Muslims. Moreover, the hijab is only a political dilemma for Muslim men. Laila Ahmad has said in many ways that hijab is the imposition of religious priesthood on women. They also held the position that traditional Islamic movements are dangerous and inimical to women.

However, the book released in April 2011 shows a change in Laila Ahmad's thinking. The book is titled 'A Quiet Revolution: The Veil's Resurgence from the Middle East to America'. Laila Ahmad says that the hijab, as the name suggests, does not represent violence, but a transition to calmness and peace. Critics consider the book to be a self-critical take on the 1992 work 'Women and Gender in Islam'.

Born into an ultra-liberal family in Cairo, Laila Ahmed remembers urban life without the presence of the hijab. They say that her mother never wore hijab. From the 1920s to the 1970s, the hijab—in many forms—was not in the mainstream of Egyptian life. Laila Ahmad traces the spread of the hijab through the history of Egypt. Viewing Egypt's own history in three parts: pre-colonial Egypt, colonized Egypt, and post-colonial Egypt, Ahmad examines how the hijab was represented within broader Islamic considerations of life in these three historical phases and in their specific political contexts. The first half of the book is description of this internal process.

In the second half suddenly Laila Ahmad leaves for America. There she examines the influence of Islamic movements on immigrant and African American Muslims in the United States and the representational nature of the hijab through the formative history of the Muslim Student Association (MSA) and the Islamic Society of North America (ISNA). Strengthened by two thousand members, they see new advances and policy developments under the leadership of Ingrid Matson - the first woman in history to lead a modern Islamic movement. She is excited to see Islamic movements evolve to include women like herself.

Laila Ahmad left Egypt in the 1960s. At that time the Islamists were oppressed by Nasser's henchmen. Like the first decades of decolonization in all Third World countries, Nasser had dreams of National Socialism. Nasser also dreamed of the same dams that Nehruvian nationalism dreamed of in the form of the Aswan Dam. The peculiarity of the third world countries is that the anti-colonial struggle and the struggle of the backward peoples have been overthrown by the nationalist elites. Such countries—in India and Egypt—were transferred to the hands of nationalist elites after decolonization. The religious contexts that actually involved the struggling masses were forgotten and new nation-states in the image of the invaders came into existence with grand claims of secularism. In India, the state of emergency invited the collapse of the national elite, while in Egypt, the defeat of the war against Israel consumed the story of the national elite. The '70s saw the return of the Islamic movement Ikhwanul Muslimoon.

Later, the Ikhwan conquered Egypt in a gradual process. Laila Ahmad says that long-term persecution has not upset the balance of the Ikhwan. Laila Ahmad says that the Ikhwan has been ready to reject Ayman al-Zawahiri's extremism since the 1960s.

Laila Ahmad studies Qutb and Zainbul Ghazzali in detail. Laila Ahmad says that the adventurous life of Zainbul Ghazali, who started her political activities as a feminist at the age of sixteen, still needs to be studied. Laila Ahmad argues that the Ikhwan did not give due consideration to Zainbul Ghazzali, who influenced the lives of Muslim women around the world. It is estimated that Zainbul Ghazzali has not received the social recognition that Ingrid Matson has received in America. The book also examines the attitudes of Islamic movements towards young people and women. It has also been observed that movements such as the Ikhwan have been slow to adopt the open methods of self-criticism that have led to the exodus of a large Islamic group of young men and women from the Ikhwan in Egypt. The reader will, of course, be surprised to know that Laila Ahmad, who criticized the Ikhwan in the first place, is the one who is doing this well-intentioned criticism. Laila Ahmad cheerfully undertakes the dialogical relationship that Islamic movements have with all the diversity of the world. Laila Ahmad greatly appreciates the organic nature of the Islamic movement, which adapts and interacts with all kinds of Islamic movements and ways of thinking. She realizes that movements like ISNA have become a learning and teaching platform for a liberal like her.

Moreover, Laila Ahmad recognizes that conventional discourses about Islam and gender also enabled the Iraq-Afghan war that cost billions of lives in the first half of this decade. 'Why is everyone concerned only about the Muslim woman?' the question is very relevant. The fact that Muslim women have concerns that do not apply to other women in the world is certainly worthy of scrutiny. Laila Abu Lughd and Saba Mahmud, who raised such questions, discuss them at length and understand the relevance of these studies that problematize the imperial anxiety and the white male gaze about the Muslim woman.

As mentioned earlier, this book tries to see the hijab through the politics of the time. However, Laila Ahmad shares some commonly shared historical conclusions about the hijab. Thus: "The meaning of hijab is not something common in society and history. The hijab seen after the 1970s is not the hijab seen in the pre-colonial era. Hijab in the pre-colonial era confined and divided women into gendered hierarchies. Later in the colonial period, the hijab became a taboo subject to be suppressed within the European worldview. As the hijab came under European control, it came to symbolize the civilized decline of Islam and the oppression of women. In the anti-colonial struggle and post-colonial conditions, the Islamic movement Ikhwan Hijab was regarded as a formidable defence armour. The hijab became a symbol of the anti-colonial struggle" (p. 212).

So what do these women—whether in Egypt or America—accomplish through the hijab? Are women re-oppressed by the hijab? Being caught by a Muslim radical patriarchy? Laila Ahmad faces such doubts with optimism.

"Initially, I was afraid of the presence of Muslim women. But I got to see these women's activism up close. I am amazed that the most authoritative voice among those talking about gender and justice is now that of Islamist women. Their struggles need to be appreciated. The conclusions I reached are more optimistic than I thought. "Happier things are happening than I thought I could achieve" (p. 303).

Laila Ahmad continues: "The 'feminist' approaches emerging today have certain characteristics. The most important thing is that devout Muslims are ready to re-read Islamic scriptures. Certainly, secular women like Nawal Saadawi have done this. But another important point is that women who have fundamental faith are involved in such initiatives. This is also helped by the situation of women's interventions for equal rights in religious institutions and leadership. This reveals the new presence and potential of Islam in the Western world" (p. 306).

The structure of the book has already been mentioned. The two-part book has eleven chapters excluding the introduction. The first chapter brings us to Egypt in the 1950s. People generally do not wear hijab. Discussions about hijab and secularism come into play here. It contains accounts of Qasim Amin's life. The statement that 'Liberation of Women was written by Mohammad Abdu along with Qasim Amin' is quite surprising. Later it is said that the book was published under the name of Qasim Amin only. The book reveals Abdu's fascination with colonialism. Subsequent chapters analyse Egypt's history from the 1920s to the 1970s. Life of Hasanul Banna, Dialogue with Banna and Zainbul Ghazzali, Leadership of Hasanul Hudaibi have also been discussed.

The first eight chapters deal with the Islamic movement in Egypt. Later, the first generation of Islamists arrived in America from the Indian subcontinent and countries including Egypt. They were activists of Jamaat-e-Islami and Ikhwanul Muslimoon. Most of the early Muslim immigrants to the United States were not Islamists or Islamist sympathizers. But a systematic, step-by-step program of action nurtured the Islamists. After 2000 there was a massive participation of youth and women in movements like ISNA.

An important point that Laila Ahmad observes is that she sees two types of hijab in such movements in the first stage. One is those who wear hijab only when they come to ISNA events. Two, ISNA's events were attended only by hijab-wearers. The ISNA then resolves such contradictions with an open approach. Such movements are taking up new discussions of gender justice and pluralism after 2000. After 9/11, young men and women in America began speaking out about justice and politics at Islamist events. They demanded justice not only in politics but also in the world across. On the contrary, they demanded equal participation of women in various organizations of Islamists. They invited not only Muslim scholars of different views but also anti-imperialist activists to the events. She kept a very critical approach towards everyone and maintained a dialogical relationship.

This is what gives Laila Ahmad new beliefs outside of mainstream liberal life. Moreover, Laila Ahmad has an ethical analysis that one does not generally have when studying Islam. In fact, the main lesson Laila Ahmad gives is this: Islamists must look at themselves in their own mirrors and criticize themselves.

IN INDIAN CONTEXT

India was the first Muslim territory conquered by the British. Therefore, the British saw India as a testing ground for bringing the Muslims under control. Later, it can be seen that the British implemented the rule in the African-Malayan regions where the Muslim rule came under the British Empire by following the Indian model. The East India Company began its rule in the Indian subcontinent through the Diwani status that the East India Company received after the Plassey War. Till then the limits of their laws were confined within their forts. With the grant of Diwani status, taxation and justice in the province of Bengal came under the purview of the East India Company. The British initially tried to rely on the legal system of the Mughal era as the power was transferred from the Mughal dynasty. To that end, the Qadhis, the traditional legal experts who implemented Islamic law during the Mughal period, were made part of the British legal system. The East India Company established the legal system by appointing them as legal officers. Brahmin Pandits were also made part of the new legal system to receive advice on Hindu law.

The British did not have to rely directly on Islamic fiqh books to implement Islamic law because they had traditional Qadis who were well-versed in Islamic jurisprudence. But gradually the East India Company tried to reduce the influence of Khadis. This is why the British, who had no Persian or Arabic base, started translating Islamic Fiqh books into English.

The first such translation was that of the Hanafi book '**Hidaya**'. Written by the 13th-century Hanafi scholar Burhanuddin Marginani, this book was the most popular book in the Hanafi madhhab in India. Since the British did not have the Arabic support, the translation was changed from the Persian translation of Hidayah to English. The Hidayah was a concise exposition of the Islamic civil and criminal market laws. However, the Hidayah did not deal with inheritance law. Following this, the British decided to translate another Hanafi book, Sirajjiya, under William Jones. This process of translation reduced Islamic jurisprudence from thousands of books to limited books.

Apart from this, the British collected each case and published it for the reference of the courts and judges. William Magnaton's first collection of such old cases (Principles and Precedents of Muhammadan Law) was published in 1824. Stare decisis (When a court faces a legal argument, if a previous court has ruled on the same or a closely related issue, then the court will make their decision in alignment with the previous court's decision) was alien to Islamic jurisprudence. This was the British common law method. Apart from that, the British also brought the method of appeal to the higher courts. Under it, the final word on Islamic law became the Privy Council, headquartered in London. The likes of Joseph Shacht point out that the resulting new legal system was at the same time an amalgamation of Islamic English legal thought. Hence the British called it Anglo-Mohammedan Law.

Initially, the East India Company Courts also relied on Islamic criminal and commercial laws as common law. Later, the First Law Commission (1834) chaired by T. B. Macaulay started discussions on making English laws common law. After the first independence movement in 1857, British-based common laws began to be widely imported into India. This was after the British Queen directly took over the administration of India from the East India Company after the First War of Independence and initiated radical administrative changes. Indian Criminal Code, 1862, Indian Transfer Act, 1882, Indian Evidence Act, 1872, Indian Contract Act, 1872, etc. are in force at present. At the same time, the British Queen announced in 1858 that the natives would have complete independence in terms of family/personal laws (Queen Victoria's Proclamation, 1858). The Queen's proclamation was sacrosanct and inviolable to the British. Hence, by the end of the nineteenth century, the scope of Islamic law was limited to the private sphere of the family/individual.

In the 1860s, the British made an effort to interpret personal laws in a broader sense. The result is the English translation of Niel Beily's Fatawa Alangiri. The collection of Hanafi fatwas known as Fatwa Alangiri or Fatwa Hind was compiled by a number of Hanafi scholars during the reign of the Mughal emperor Aurangzeb at his behest. Only the parts covered by the Nilee Beily personal rules have been translated into English. It was published under the title 'Digest of Muhammadan Law'. It was during this period that the traditional experts, the Qadhis, were completely expelled from the judicial system. With this, the authorship of Islamic personal law was transferred to modernly trained judges and English translations. "What happens to the Shari'a is best described not as curtailment but as transmutation. Talal Asad's view that it is rendered into a subdivision of legal norms (fiqh) that are authorized and maintained by the centralizing state is confirmed by the history of Islamic laws in India.

The influence of British laws was very evident in the Islamic personal laws that were transferred to British authority. Colonial court judgments therefore often sided with traditional sources of personal law. The Waqf-ul-Aulad controversy was a major controversy during the colonial period based on whether modern courts had complete authority over Islamic personal law. The British Supreme Court, the Privy Council, ruled that *Waqf-ul-Aulad* was invalid under Islamic law and that the Privy Council had the final word on the matter. The British judge Hob House announced such a verdict in 1893. At the same time, according to traditional Islamic sources, it was not forbidden to make waqf to one's own family.

The rule against perpetuities was against the British market law, which allowed private individuals to become beneficiaries of the property. Muslims were unwilling to accept the British Supreme Court's authority on Islamic law. Following this, Muslims organized large protests in India. The Indian National Congress and the Muslim League came up with resolutions against the Privy Council.

Ulama such as Shibli Noumani collected the fatwas of Islamic scholars from around the world to justify the acceptance of *Waqf Aulad*. Following this, Muhammad Ali Jinnah's Waqf Validation Bill was brought in 1911 and in 1913 it was officially approved. According to this law, the family waqf of Muslims is valid under Islamic personal law. This was the first codification of Islamic personal law in Indian history. It was also the first time in the history of the Privy Council itself that a judgment was overturned. This was seen as a decisive victory in the political history of the Muslims.

In post-independence India, the judgment of the Supreme Court in the Shah Banu case once again raised the question of who the author of Islamic personal law is. According to the Supreme Court's judgment, the alimony of the divorced ex-wife is the responsibility of the ex-husband. due to the protest by misinformed clergy and vested politicians, Rajiv Gandhi's government overturned the Supreme Court's decision, thus squashing an important chance to reform Islamic law according to modern needs. Political class always used Islamic law as a bargaining tool stalling the timely modification of Muslim law.

The fact is that there is no tendency to impose civil laws in any democratic country in the world today. There is a tendency in developed countries to allow even immigrants freedom in their civil laws. Countries that do not have democratic governments and such civil laws allow citizens and immigrants the right to live according to their civil laws. History also testifies that even the most anti-democratic colonial regimes did not encroach on indigenous peoples' civil liberties. It can be seen that in pre-modern history too, a totally alien arrangement was to encroach upon the freedom of the civil laws of different societies. Recognizing this fact, the 21st Law Commission proposed that personal laws in India are indicators of democracy and there is no need for a uniform civil code. So, any such attempt in the name of unification has to be seen as a challenge to human freedom and history itself.

At the same time, efforts should be made by the Muslim community itself to reform themselves. while the nation is shedding its colonial legacy, if Islamic law lags it will be stuck in anachronism. It's high time for Muslim leadership to think about ways to free away from colonial laws to modernity. Many Arabian countries and progressive Muslim laws in Muslim countries show the way.

In the churning times, if Muslims don't shed social conservatism it will culminate in disaster. It's precious to remember that the root cause of Partition was religious conservatism of Muslims when the global system advanced in terms of modernity and liberty.

CHAPTER IX

Colonial Epistemology And Shaping Of Muslim Personal Law

India has seen the essence of Islamic law since the conquest of Sindh by Muhammad ibn Qasim in 712 AD. However, the law was not established until after the reign of Qutbuddin Ibn Bakr in the early 13th century. The Mughal kings followed Hanafi Madhhabs. The first authentic Islamic law book found in India was the Hanafi Law Book, Hidaya, written in the 12th century by Burhanuddin Marginani, who was born in present day Russia and Turkey. Later, in the 13th century, a Shia scholar by the name of Najmuddin al-Hilli wrote a book on Shia law entitled Sharaul Islam. The Fatawa Alangiri, a collection of fatwas issued by scholars up to the time of Aurangzeb during his reign, was written in the 17th century because of the fact that judgments based on principles were more useful than books containing abstract principles. 'Hidaya' was translated from Arabic into Persian and later into English. 'Fatawa Alangiri' and 'Sharul Islam' were published in English by a judge named Bailey as 'Bailey's Digest'. These three books were written in India to understand Islamic law. These books trace the roots of Muslim personal law in India even today. The Shafis also have an English translation of the book Minhaj-u-Talibeen.

It has long been accepted that Hindu law and Muslim law are inextricably linked to their religions. As a result, when Muslim law was applied to Muslims, Hindu law was extended to Hindus by the Mughal emperors. This policy was not re-introduced by the British except to be followed later. When the East India Company began trading and governing in the 17th century AD, the Hindu-Muslim communities were given the freedom to obey their religious personal rules in all matters. According to Regulation II, passed in 1772, cases relating to rituals, inheritance, marriage, caste, and caste (here caste means religion), according to the Qur'an, belong to Muslims, and 'Shastra' to Hindus. It was suggested that the verdict should be decided accordingly.

Maulvis were appointed to teach the Qur'an and Pandits to teach science. This measure has been in place for a long time. In all but the above cases, caste and religion were judged in accordance with the principles of justice of the English.

When the British took over India from the East India Company in 1858, the 'authority' of British law was tightened. The British Parliament passed the Prohibition of Slavery Act in 1843 and the Caste Disability Prevention Act in 1850. One forbade enslaving human beings. A person of another caste or religion does not lose the inheritance and inheritance rights under civil law. They implemented both these Acts in India. Since the enactment of the Indian Penal Code in 1860, the same penal code has been enacted throughout India. With the implementation of all these communal remedies, Muslims were unable to enforce their own law on these issues.

In 1861, the High Court was established in three places, Bombay, Calcutta and Madras. In 1872, Evidence Act was enacted for India in accordance with British principles. Since then, Muslims have lost the Islamic proof of law. The Act, passed by Parliament in 1887, required that when adjudicating matters relating to the property, marriage and religion of a Muslim, all other parts of the body should be applied except those which have been altered or removed by law. Relevant in this context is the fact that the British law amended the Islamic property law, which states that the property of a Muslim cannot be given to a non - Muslim, but the property rights are not destroyed by caste change. But British law did not interfere in marriage and religious ceremonies. They respected traditions and customs. It is a fact that the opposition to rituals is still prevalent among Muslims to the extent that some un-Islamic practices are accepted.

With the establishment of the High Courts in 1860, the office of Court Adviser to the *Maulvis* and Scholars came to an end; the presence of lawyers with legal training in the courts was required. The system in which the *Maulvi* was replaced by lawyers had both advantages and disadvantages. The Maulvis were still strict theorists. They were not sure of worldly contact or procedure. The language they knew was unknown to the British judges or to the language the judges knew. The number of cases had increased. Their diversity and complexity increased. From the 1880s to the 7th century, India can be said to have been the golden age of Muslim personal law.

During this period, modern jurists such as Justice Mahmoud, Justice Amir Ali, Justice Abdur Rahim, Barrister AFM Abdurrahman, and others echoed what was available in Arabic and Persian. Justice Tayyibji and others made valuable contributions to the development of Muslim personal law. They were able to access the original texts in Arabic. But British judges were amazed at the complexity of Islamic law and the difficulty of interpreting it from its original sources. A senior British judge once said in a ruling that he would have been glad if the Muslim legal issue had come before him and he could not have escaped without making a decision. Codification has taken place in only a small part of Muslim personal law.

Family Waqf Validation Act of 1913, Shariah Act of 1937, Fasq Act of 1939, Waqf Act of 1854, Mappila Marriage Act of 1918, Mappila Vasyat (will) Act of 1928, Kashmir Muslim Maher (dowry) Act of 1920, The laws were codified in 1938 as the Kachimeman Act and in 1949 as the Muslim Marriage and Talaq Registration Act (for Odisha, Assam, Bihar and West Bengal only) and the null and void Khasi Act of 1880. The most important of these, the Shariah Act, is described below.

Except for the parts contained in the Acts, the rest are '*Hidayah*' for Hanafi law and '*Minhaj*' for Shafi'i law. Because the Hanafis are in the majority, court decisions are more in accordance with Hanafi law. Today's lawyers and judges do not go into the original texts. They usually look only at past Privy Council rulings and now Supreme Court rulings and High Court rulings.

The Privy Council had imposed some wrong judgments in Muslim law. In 1894 they annulled the family *Waqf*. The Prophet (peace and blessings of Allah be upon him) allowed and encouraged it. The British judges did not heed Justice Amir Ali's first ruling in a judgment that it should not therefore be invalidated. The judges rejected Amir Ali's opinion because they could not believe that the Prophet (peace and blessings of Allah be upon him) did not allow property to be permanently held by charity, but was allowed to do so in the name of 'dharma'. (Abdul Fatah Case). The Family Waqf Validation Act of 1913 was passed in India as a result of the agitation of the Indian Muslim community against this erroneous judgment.

In 1897 another erroneous judgment was made. Amir Ali argued that the Qur'an commands that a woman who has lost her husband stay in her husband's house for a year and protect her, citing Chapter 2, Verse 240 of the Qur'an. The judges did not accept. The reason given is strange. They do not have to look at what the Qur'an says. The reason given was that they did not see such a right in 'Hidayah' or 'Imam'. (Kulsumbi case). The Privy Council disagreed with Justice Mahmoud's ruling that Shiites should not make waqf by will; The reason given was that they were not prepared to accept any new principles which the ancients had not stated. Their judgments in religious matters did not address the 'right' aspects of the subject. They were based on rules. However, Such judgments later became law.

When a dispute arose in the Bombay High Court in 1871 over whether three statements in one breath could result in three divorces, it was counted as three Talaqs, saying that such statements had been considered as three divorces for 75 years.

When the issue of whether Ahmadis were Muslims came up in the Madras High Court in 1921, a British judge and Justice Krishnan from Kannur ruled that they were Muslims. Justice Krishna Iyer had also passed a similar order in the Kerala High Court. It is doubtful whether the verdicts would have been the same if the Muslim judges had been in the judicial chair. These judgments indicate that those with religious knowledge and perspectives are more capable of deciding religious issues. Hindu judges have the same ability in cases involving Hindu issues.

Many un-Islamic laws in Muslim personal law have been passed on to ritual force. The law of marriage, which has been observed for centuries among the Mappilas, and some of the Hindu customs that existed in the Kachimeman, Khoja and Bora sects. In Kashmir, the law denies women property rights and is content with mere protection (this has been changed with the abrogation of Article 370). These were all part of the Muslim Personal Law. The Shariah Act passed in 1937, is an important milestone in Muslim personal law. The Act declares that if the parties are Muslims, even if there is a contradictory custom or custom, property of non-possession, property for women, property by contract or gift, marriage, divorce, protection, *Mahr*, guardianship, alms, including divorce and divorce, *Sihar, Qul'* and *Mubara*; Cases between Muslims on matters of trust and *Waqf* of religious institutions should be decided in accordance with Shariah principles. Those who have written to the authorities stating that they wish to take advantage of the Act will be able to abstain from adoption and possession of the entire property in addition to the above matters.

The reason for this is that in the Kachimeman-Khoja communities, there was this un-Islamic adoption as a custom and the practice of confiscating all property. They were able to enjoy the benefits of this act by not adopting it freely if they wished, and by doing so only in accordance with the Shariah. The following year, the Kachimemans passed another act in 1938, deviating from these un-Islamic customary rules and enacting the Shariah Act. The Khojas have a mixture of some Muslim and some Hindu laws. They also follow some Sunni laws and some Shia laws. The Shariah Act does not apply to Kashmir Muslims. Because this is the law of India except for Kashmir (changed after abrogation of Article 370).

The Malabar Mappilas practised certain Hindu rules in ancient times. They possessed all their possessions like the Hindus. Even sovereign property was not inherited by the heirs except the son-in-law after death. This situation was amended by two Provincial Acts. In 1918, the Matriline Act was passed. As a result, the inherited property was given to the heirs under Muslim law. With the passage of the Mappila Vasyat (will) Act in 1928, only one-third of Muslim law allows them to make a will. The property, which was divided according to the custom of marriage, was passed to the heirs according to Muslim law. After the Shariah Act, no un-Islamic practice was allowed to comply with property matters. The nuptial system should no longer be created.

The Shariah Act is only a declaration act. It does not elaborate on the Shariah principles of the issues raised in it. As this applies to all Muslims, the different legal aspects of Shia, Sunni, Shafi, Hanafi, etc., and sects remain unchanged and they can obey their own sectarian rules. The Fasq Act (marriage Dissolution by women) of 1939 has taken a more effective approach in this regard. This Act applies to all Muslims, regardless of Sunni-Shia or Madhhab distinctions. It enumerates the legal principles of *Fasq*. Therefore, they can be known to everyone. The Shariah Act required so.

Other Muslim countries have codified Sharia law. In India, codification came into force after the Shariah Act was enacted (two years later) under the Fasq Act. It became the most appropriate and useful. Shariah law requires its codification. For this, it is sufficient to explain and reconstruct the Shariah Act.

CHAPTER X

Muslim Personal Law In India: A Historical Account

Muslim family law in India has undergone significant transformation over the centuries, shaped by a complex interplay of religious doctrines, colonial legacies, socio-political dynamics, and legal reforms. As a pluralistic society with a significant Muslim population, India's approach to Muslim family law has been marked by attempts to balance Islamic legal principles with the demands of a secular, democratic framework. This essay delves into the historical evolution and legislative reforms of Muslim family laws in India, exploring the role of colonial rule, post-independence legal developments, and contemporary challenges in the pursuit of justice and equality.

Historical Context: The Pre-Colonial Period

Before the advent of British colonial rule, Muslim family law in India was primarily governed by Sharia, or Islamic law, as interpreted by the various schools of Islamic jurisprudence. The application of these laws varied across regions and communities, influenced by local customs and the specific legal traditions of the Hanafi school, which was predominant among Indian Muslims. During the Mughal period, the Qazi (Islamic judge) system was central to the administration of Muslim personal law, handling matters related to marriage, divorce, inheritance, and maintenance.

The Mughal rulers allowed considerable autonomy to religious communities in the administration of their personal laws, a practice that continued under successive regimes. Muslim family law during this period was characterized by a degree of flexibility, with local customs and interpretations often blending with religious doctrines. The legal system was largely decentralized, with the application of law being contingent on the interpretations of local

Qazis, leading to variations in legal practices across the subcontinent.

The Impact Of British Colonial Rule

The arrival of the British in the 18th century marked a turning point in the administration of Muslim family law in India. The British colonial authorities sought to consolidate their control over the diverse legal systems of India, leading to the codification and standardization of laws. This process had profound implications for Muslim personal law.

In 1772, Warren Hastings, the then Governor-General of India, introduced the system of applying the Sharia in matters of personal law for Muslims through the Bengal Regulation Act. This regulation established that in cases of marriage, inheritance, and religious usage, the law of the Quran would be applied to Muslims. However, this codification process often involved selective and rigid interpretations of Islamic law, stripping it of the flexibility that had characterized its earlier application. The colonial courts, often presided over by British judges unfamiliar with the nuances of Islamic jurisprudence, relied heavily on the opinions of Islamic scholars and translators, further solidifying a more static interpretation of Muslim family law.

The most significant colonial-era legislation affecting Muslim family law was the Shariat Application Act of 1937. This Act was introduced in response to demands from Muslim leaders who sought to replace customary laws with Sharia in matters of personal law. The Act mandated that in all questions relating to personal status, the courts would apply the Muslim Personal Law (Shariat), effectively overruling the application of customary laws that had been prevalent among various Muslim communities. The Shariat Application Act marked a significant step in the consolidation of Muslim family law in India, but it also entrenched certain patriarchal interpretations of Islamic law, particularly concerning women's rights in marriage, divorce, and inheritance.

Post-Independence Legal Developments

The partition of India in 1947 and the subsequent creation of Pakistan marked a watershed moment in the history of Muslim family law in the subcontinent. In independent India, the question of Muslim personal law became a focal point in the broader debate over the role of religion in the legal and political life of the newly established secular state.

The Indian Constitution, adopted in 1950, provided for the continuation of personal laws for different religious communities, including Muslims. Article 44 of the Directive Principles of State Policy, however, envisaged the establishment of a Uniform Civil Code (UCC), which would bring all citizens under a common set of personal laws, irrespective of religion. The UCC remains one of the most contentious issues in Indian politics, with strong opposition from Muslim leaders and communities who view it as a threat to their religious identity and autonomy.

Despite the constitutional provision for the continuation of Muslim personal law, the post-independence period saw significant judicial interventions and legislative reforms aimed at addressing gender inequality within Muslim family law. The landmark case of Shah Bano in 1985 highlighted the tensions between religious personal law and constitutional principles of gender justice. In this case, the Supreme Court of India ruled that Shah Bano, a divorced Muslim woman, was entitled to alimony under the secular criminal law provisions of the Code of Criminal Procedure (CrPC), despite the stipulations of Muslim personal law that limited maintenance to the period of iddat (the waiting period after divorce).

The Shah Bano judgment sparked widespread controversy and protests from Muslim leaders, leading the government to enact the Muslim Women (Protection of Rights on Divorce) Act in 1986. This Act sought to nullify the Supreme Court's ruling by limiting the liability of Muslim men to provide maintenance beyond the iddat period. The Act was criticized by women's rights activists and secularists as a regressive step that undermined the rights of Muslim women and reinforced patriarchal interpretations of Islamic law. However, it also highlighted the deep-seated tensions between religious law and state intervention in matters of personal law.

Legislative Reforms And Contemporary Challenges

In recent decades, there has been a growing movement within India for the reform of Muslim family law to align it more closely with constitutional principles of equality and justice. Women's rights groups, legal scholars, and progressive Muslim voices have been at the forefront of this movement, advocating for changes that address gender-based discrimination within Muslim personal law.

One of the most significant developments in this regard has been the campaign against triple talaq (Instant divorce), a practice that allows a Muslim man to unilaterally divorce his wife by uttering the word "talaq" (divorce) three times in succession. This practice, though not universally accepted within Islamic jurisprudence, was recognized under Indian Muslim personal law and was often used to the detriment of women's rights.

In 2017, the Supreme Court of India delivered a historic judgment in the Shayara Bano case, declaring the practice of triple talaq unconstitutional. The Court held that triple talaq violated the fundamental rights of Muslim women and was not an essential practice of Islam. The ruling was widely hailed as a victory for women's rights and a significant step towards gender justice within Muslim family law.

In response to the Supreme Court's judgment, the Indian government enacted the Muslim Women (Protection of Rights on Marriage) Act in 2019, which criminalized the practice of triple talaq and provided for legal safeguards to protect the rights of Muslim women. The Act was seen as a landmark reform in Muslim family law in India, though it also faced criticism from some quarters for criminalizing a civil matter and potentially leading to the incarceration of Muslim men.

Despite these reforms, challenges remain in achieving comprehensive legislative reform in Muslim family law in India. The issue of polygamy, for instance, continues to be a contentious one. While the practice of polygamy is permitted under Muslim personal law, it has been increasingly criticized for its impact on women's rights and its incompatibility with the constitutional principles of equality. Women's rights groups have called for legislative action to restrict or prohibit polygamy, but such reforms have faced resistance from conservative Muslim leaders who view them as an infringement on religious freedom.

Another area of concern is the law of inheritance under Muslim personal law, which provides for unequal shares for men and women. While Muslim women have the right to inherit property, their share is often half that of their male counterparts. This disparity has been the subject of debate and legal challenges, with calls for reform to ensure gender equality in inheritance rights. However, the issue remains unresolved, with strong opposition from traditionalists who argue that the unequal shares are rooted in Islamic principles that cannot be altered.

The Role Of Civil Society And Progressive Muslim Voices

The push for legislative reform in Muslim family law in India has been significantly influenced by the efforts of civil society organizations, women's rights groups, and progressive Muslim scholars and activists. These groups have played a crucial role in advocating for changes to discriminatory practices and in raising awareness about the need for gender justice within the framework of Islamic law.

Organizations such as the All India Muslim Women's Personal Law Board (AIMWPLB) and the Bharatiya Muslim Mahila Andolan (BMMA) have been at the forefront of campaigns for reform, particularly on issues such as triple talaq, polygamy, and inheritance rights. These groups have engaged in legal advocacy, public awareness campaigns, and dialogue with religious leaders to promote a more progressive interpretation of Muslim personal law that aligns with constitutional values.

Progressive Muslim scholars and jurists have also contributed to the reform discourse by offering alternative interpretations of Islamic law that emphasize principles of justice, equality, and human dignity. These scholars argue that Islamic jurisprudence is not monolithic and that there is room for reform within the tradition. They advocate for a contextual and dynamic approach to interpreting Sharia that takes into account the changing needs of society and the evolving understanding of gender relations.

The Debate Over Uniform Civil Code

The debate over the Uniform Civil Code (UCC) remains one of the most polarizing issues in the discourse on Muslim family law in India. Proponents of the UCC argue that a common set of personal laws for all citizens, irrespective of religion, is essential for ensuring equality and justice. They contend that the existence of separate personal laws for different religious communities perpetuates gender inequality and undermines the secular fabric of the Indian state.

Opponents of the UCC, however, view it as a threat to religious freedom and minority rights. Muslim leaders and organizations have consistently opposed the implementation of a UCC, arguing that it would infringe on their right to practice their religion and would homogenize India's diverse cultural and religious traditions. They argue that reform within Muslim personal law should come from within the community and should respect the religious beliefs

Legal Pluralism Of Islamic Sharia And Colonial Codification Of Muslim Personal Law

"Abbasid caliph Abu Ja'far al-Mansur was asked by the minister and literary genius Ibn al-Muqafah to formulate a civil law code to unify Sharia jurisprudence for administrative transparency. Caliph Mansoor took such an opinion seriously in view of the correctness of administration and decided to convert 'Muwatta' by Ibn Malik into a law book as the most accurately codified Fiqh book of the time. Caliph Mansoor made that request to Imam Malik, the author of the Muwatta, during a Hajj: "I wish to send a copy of this book of yours to every town and instruct them to accept the laws just because of what is in it. You are from Medina. The knowledge of Madinah is authentic". Rejecting the Caliph's demand, Imam Malik's response was: "Ameer ul Mu'mineen (leader of the believers), you should not do that. Each nation has received different opinions, heard different hadiths, and lived according to what each of them had come to them from different kinds of legal views among the companions of the Prophet and among their descendants. It would not be appropriate to dismiss their views. It is better to let the people act as they act, and let each locality adopt the laws according to the laws it has received, and leave them to their own ways."

Islamic Sharia And Civil Society

Imam Malik's interest in rejecting the Caliph's demand to codify and determine the Islamic Sharia in a one-dimensional manner was to stop the power-interest, and in each case, the scholars of the respective time and land should determine the solutions for the problems. After that, it was not until the nineteenth century that anyone dared to prepare a unified law book or penal code called 'Islamic Sharia'. Rather, it existed through numerous texts, circumstantial interpretations, served civil society, and pluralized and practised Islamic jurisprudence in through multiple approaches.

The multi-dialectical nature of the Sharia was not compatible with nineteenth-century colonial power interests. The features of decentralized Sharia were not amenable to the colonial administration and they tried to subsume it under their authority. Joseph Shatt , Ignaz Goldsier, and Snook were pioneers in the project. Orientalists and other viceroys of various Muslim lands claimed that the Islamic legal system was imprecise and demanded reform. The most important characteristic of the Sharia was that it was not subordinated to the interests of state power anywhere in history. The rules of Sharia were developed by scholars who acted as independent bodies. But in contrast to that, in European nations, laws existed as an exercise of power by the ruling class. Therefore, law-making systems remained part of the state in the European system of governance.

The Sharia was operationalised by being integrated into civil society and influencing every part of their lives. It was therefore in many respects a system that was more closely related to civil society than to the state. Wa'il Hallaq says:

"Shariah was not meant to be a problem-solving mechanism. It has greatly influenced all aspects of the society, economic, moral, spiritual and cultural. This is where Sharia differs from the modern legal system. Sharia takes shape and evolves from whatever society it was formed to serve. In that way, ordinary citizens are constantly aware of the legal system and become a constant part of their daily lives. The fuqaha/muftis were constantly imparting legal knowledge to the society."

Colonial Codes And The Open Legal System

In Franz Kafka's short story 'Before the Law', the law is presented as inaccessible to the common people and distant from them. The main character in 'The Trial', who does not know what wrong he has been punished for, and the character in 'Before the

Law', who has to wait until he dies at the door of the law to know what the law is, have the same problem. However, it arises from the fact that the modern legal system keeps a distance from society. The crisis of law standing apart from society, which Kafka reveals, does not therefore arise in the Sharia, which constantly interacts with society in all its aspects.

Shariah was understood as a social and personal relationship between the people and the legal system rather than a tool to rule and control. Sharia was aligned with the legal positivist HLA Hart's observation that 'law is given its legitimacy by its sociality'. Khalid Abul Fadl writes:

"The basis of Islamic jurisprudence was the principle that laws should stand for human good, administration of justice, and classification of good and evil. Sharia was based on the (independent) interpretations of the text by scholars, as opposed to the modern secular system based on laws set by the state. They [scholars] maintained that all such interpretations were at the same time different readings, and therefore all of them were correct and any of them could be accepted."

The European legal system existed as 'codes' such as the Dutch National Code, the British Penal Code and the Napoleonic Code. Therefore, all of them were recorded and determined in different books, and they were separated as a separate field from the society by building special buildings for management. But there were no 'special spaces' in Islamic history to enforce Sharia, find legal solutions to problems and air grievances. Sharia rules were discussed in the homes of scholars, the needy, in mosques, in markets, and in royal assemblies. There was no specific text to highlight that 'this is Sharia Law'. Because in Shariah, the book was not important, rather it was the person seeking legal protection and their environment. The modern liberal approach to such an open legal system can be read in the words of an American judge: "We are not Muslim Qadis who sit under a tree and interpret the book in their hand to dictate the law as it seems."

Modernity And Sharia: From Ottoman Egypt To Anglo-Muhammadan Law

Orientalists and colonial authorities were interested in codifying Islamic laws by proposing to reject the uniqueness of the Islamic Sharia outside the European system. They therefore tried to rewrite the existing Sharia systems in other Muslim countries based on their own system. Thus, the first official codification of Islamic Sharia took place in India under the British Raj. It was creating a hybrid legal system under Governor Warren Hastings. By British Orientalist Sir William Jones under the directive of viceroy, the British company began efforts to make Muslim and Hindu laws into a unified code. To codify Muslim law, texts from the Hanafi Madhhab such as Margini's Hidaya in 1791 were translated by Charles Hamilton , Sirajiyah in 1792, and Fatawa Alamgiriyya in 1865 by Nile Bailey, which formed the 'Anglo Muhammadan Law' in 1860. But in Anglo-Muhammadan Law, the 'Anglo' lock prevailed over the 'Muhammadan' Law. This led to the later colonial Muslim law of 1937, the 'Muslim Personal Law Application Act', which made Sharia exclusively personal/civil law.

By the 20th century, the colonial power had completely established the supremacy of the European legal system in the monetary and criminal-penal laws in the Muslim world. Thus, colonialism reduced Sharia to personal laws only. By the 1880s, there was a proposal to codify the Sharia in Egypt, and a group of Qadis and British officials drafted the Muslim Personal Law incorporating the dominant views of the Hanafi madhhab. By the 1930s, the French regime had similarly formulated a Sharia code in Morocco. Similarly, in 1873, the code created by the Dutch administration in Java, incorporating Sharia and local customs, was almost identical to the Dutch National Code.

Then, what happened when the Shariah was codified by the colonial authorities in various places was the rejection of the most important features of the Sharia, namely pluralism. The 'Personal Sharia Laws' codified one of many opinions and reduced the painstaking process of 'Iftaa (giving legal opinion) to one that any officer could do by reading a single book. In addition, colonial regimes were able to codify Sharia law under state control. However, that process created many legal, social and religious crises and caused the term Sharia to be misunderstood.

According to Mark Fathi Masood, head of the University of California Law School, the rise of religious fundamentalists and the misuse of Sharia is traced to the Sharia system created by the colonial authorities. He observes that bringing Sharia under the authority of the state is exactly what the fundamentalists have done in countries like Iran, Saudi Arabia, Somalia, and Nigeria, which is the reverse and consequence of colonial interest itself.

Amira Zahri Sombol explores the point in the current political context. She writes that it was very easy for a woman to get a divorce during the Ottoman period and that the Sharia itself had provisions to implement many possibilities for the good of women. But they observed that in post-colonial Egypt, obtaining a divorce has become a difficult legal process for a woman, and divorce is granted only if it can be proven on the basis of strong evidence or by the husband's own confession that the wife has been subjected to severe torture. While sexually assaulted women were protected and compensated under the early modern Sharia system, they were often punished or euthanized by their families in the post-colonial system. In the same way, Saba Mahmoud states in the book 'Religious Difference in the Secular Age' that the rights of minorities were protected under the Ottoman Sharia system in Egypt, but the modern secular Egyptian system has failed to protect the rights of minorities.

The Possibilities Of Sharia Beyond Foucauldian Laws

For Michel Foucault, 'laws are instruments of power'. Law reinforces the relationship of power through all its institutions and materials. He points out that laws are not just certain principles or directives, but an ever-evolving exercise of power. Ibrahim Musa's understanding of colonial codification based on Foucault's arguments is as follows:

"The colonial powers secured power not only through military-political-economic power, but also by imposing their legal wisdom on the colonized. The consequence is that even after independence, the colonized are trapped under the legal system of the same colonial powers that oppressed them."

Therefore, it is not possible to formulate and understand Sharia in terms of European legal theories, since Islamic Sharia exists in contrast to the centralized European legal system. As Derrida observes in 'Force of Law: The Mystical Foundation of Authority' with Walter Benjamin in mind, law in the European system has always functioned only for the survival of the 'law/state'. Its primary objective is always, 'its own self-sustainment'. Hence its mission is to 'maintain established authority without crisis'. So, the basis of modern laws is always authority.

But since the Shariah, in contrast, essentially aims at 'the moral formation of civil society and the protection of rights', its basic characteristic is 'decentralization of power'. Thus, it never becomes 'absolute' in itself like modern laws. Rather, Islamic Shariah is a decentralized one, constantly in the process of 'becoming', renewing itself and renewing society through dealings with social conditions 'external' to it.

CHAPTER XII

From Imperialism To Democracy: The Dilemmas Of Sharia

India was the first Muslim territory conquered by the British. Therefore, the British saw India as a testing ground for bringing the Muslims under control. Later, it can be seen that the British implemented the rule in the African-Malayan regions where the Muslim rule came under the British Empire by following the Indian model. The East India Company began its rule in the Indian subcontinent through the Diwani status that the East India Company received after the Plassey War. Till then the limits of their laws were confined within their forts. With the grant of Diwani status, taxation and justice in the province of Bengal came under the purview of the East India Company. The British initially tried to rely on the legal system of the Mughal era as the power was transferred from the Mughal dynasty. To that end, the Qadhis, the traditional legal experts who implemented Islamic law during the Mughal period, were made part of the British legal system. The East India Company established the legal system by appointing them as legal officers. Brahmin Pandits were also made part of the new legal system to receive advice on Hindu law.

The British did not have to rely directly on Islamic fiqh books to implement Islamic law because they had traditional Qadis who were well-versed in Islamic jurisprudence. But gradually the East India Company tried to reduce the influence of Khadis. This is why the British, who had no Persian or Arabic base, started translating Islamic Fiqh books into English.

The first such translation was that of the Hanafi book 'Hidaya'. Written by the 13th-century Hanafi scholar Burhanuddin Marginani, this book was the most popular book in the Hanafi madhhab in India. Since the British did not have the Arabic support, the translation was changed from the Persian translation of Hidayah to English. The Hidayah was a concise exposition of the Islamic civil and criminal market laws. However, the Hidayah did not deal with inheritance law. Following this, the British decided to translate another Hanafi book, Sirajjiya, under William Jones. This process of translation reduced Islamic jurisprudence from thousands of books to limited books.

Apart from this, the British collected each case and published it for the reference of the courts and judges. William Magnaton's first collection of such old cases (Principles and Precedents of Muhammadan Law) was published in 1824. Stare decisis (When a court faces a legal argument, if a previous court has ruled on the same or a closely related issue, then the court will make their decision in alignment with the previous court's decision) was alien to Islamic jurisprudence. This was the British common law method. Apart from that, the British also brought the method of appeal to the higher courts. Under it, the final word on Islamic law became the Privy Council, headquartered in London. The likes of Joseph Shacht point out that the resulting new legal system was at the same time an amalgamation of Islamic English legal thought. Hence the British called it Anglo-Mohammedan Law.

Initially, the East India Company Courts also relied on Islamic criminal and commercial laws as common law. Later, the First Law Commission (1834) chaired by T. B. Macaulay started discussions on making English laws common law. After the first independence movement in 1857, British-based common laws began to be widely imported into India. This was after the British Queen directly took over the administration of India from the East India Company after the First War of Independence and initiated radical administrative changes. Indian Criminal Code, 1862, Indian Transfer Act, 1882, Indian Evidence Act, 1872, Indian Contract Act, 1872, etc. are in force at present. At the same time, the British Queen announced in 1858 that the natives would have complete independence in terms of family/personal laws (Queen Victoria's Proclamation, 1858). The Queen's proclamation was sacrosanct and inviolable to the

British. Hence, by the end of the nineteenth century, the scope of Islamic law was limited to the private sphere of the family/individual.

In the 1860s, the British made an effort to interpret personal laws in a broader sense. The result is the English translation of Niel Beily's Fatawa Alangiri. The collection of Hanafi fatwas known as Fatwa Alangiri or Fatwa Hind was compiled by a number of Hanafi scholars during the reign of the Mughal emperor Aurangzeb at his behest. Only the parts covered by the Nilee Beily personal rules have been translated into English. It was published under the title 'Digest of Muhammadan Law'. It was during this period that the traditional experts, the Qadhis, were completely expelled from the judicial system. With this, the authorship of Islamic personal law was transferred to modernly trained judges and English translations. "What happens to the Shari'a is best described not as curtailment but as transmutation. Talal Asad's view that it is rendered into a subdivision of legal norms (fiqh) that are authorized and maintained by the centralizing state is confirmed by the history of Islamic laws in India.

The influence of British laws was very evident in the Islamic personal laws that were transferred to British authority. Colonial court judgments therefore often sided with traditional sources of personal law. The Waqf-ul-Aulad controversy was a major controversy during the colonial period based on whether modern courts had complete authority over Islamic personal law. The British Supreme Court, the Privy Council, ruled that *Waqf-ul-Aulad* was invalid under Islamic law and that the Privy Council had the final word on the matter. The British judge Hob House announced such a verdict in 1893. At the same time, according to traditional Islamic sources, it was not forbidden to make waqf to one's own family.

The rule against perpetuities was against the British market law, which allowed private individuals to become beneficiaries of the property. Muslims were unwilling to accept the British Supreme Court's authority on Islamic law. Following this, Muslims organized large protests in India. The Indian National Congress and the Muslim League came up with resolutions against the Privy Council.

Ulama such as Shibli Noumani collected the fatwas of Islamic scholars from around the world to justify the acceptance of *Waqf Aulad*. Following this, Muhammad Ali Jinnah's Waqf Validation Bill was brought in 1911 and in 1913 it was officially approved. According to this law, the family waqf of Muslims is valid under Islamic personal law. This was the first codification of Islamic personal law in Indian history. It was also the first time in the history of the Privy Council itself that a judgment was overturned. This was seen as a decisive victory in the political history of the Muslims.

In post-independence India, the judgment of the Supreme Court in the Shah Banu case once again raised the question of who the author of Islamic personal law is. According to the Supreme Court's judgment, the alimony of the divorced ex-wife is the responsibility of the ex-husband. due to the protest by misinformed clergy and vested politicians, Rajiv Gandhi's government overturned the Supreme Court's decision, thus squashing an important chance to reform Islamic law according to modern needs. Political class always used Islamic law as a bargaining tool stalling the timely modification of Muslim law.

The fact is that there is no tendency to impose civil laws in any democratic country in the world today. There is a tendency in developed countries to allow even immigrants freedom in their civil laws. Countries that do not have democratic governments and such civil laws allow citizens and immigrants the right to live according to their civil laws. History also testifies that even the most anti-democratic colonial regimes did not encroach on indigenous peoples' civil liberties. It can be seen that in pre-modern history too, a totally alien arrangement was to encroach upon the freedom of the civil laws of different societies. Recognizing this fact, the 21st Law Commission proposed that personal laws in India are indicators of democracy and there is no need for a uniform civil code. So, any such attempt in the name of unification has to be seen as a challenge to human freedom and history itself.

At the same time, efforts should be made by the Muslim community itself to reform themselves. while the nation is shedding its colonial legacy, if Islamic law lags it will be stuck in anachronism. It's high time for Muslim leadership to think about ways to free away from colonial laws to modernity. Many Arabian countries and progressive Muslim laws in Muslim countries show the way. In the churning times, if Muslims don't shed social conservatism it will culminate in disaster. It's precious to remember that the root cause of Partition was religious conservatism of Muslims when the global system advanced in terms of modernity and liberty.

CHAPTER XIII

Islamic Revival Movement In Contemporary India And Approaches To Islamic Law

In the last century, Islamic renaissance movements all over the world emerged as a response to the many problems and challenges that Muslims in particular and the people of the world in general were facing, both nationally and internationally. Islamic movements have formed their field of action by correcting the ideological and practical failures that occurred in Muslim society through the continuous movement of history and pointing out the problems that have affected world civilization. Religious content, political analysis, and social representation are naturally deeply reflected in the language and style of the Islamic movement.

The West has met this representation of Islam with the misnomer of 'political Islam'. Thus, the West rejected the political experiences of Islam and rejected the new developments. No matter how advanced secular modernity and liberal democracy were, the gates of all its possibilities were closed to Islam. It was here that the historical fate of the revivalist movements was determined. Analysing modern myths based on Islamic thought and instilling confidence in the Muslim Ummah to confront it is no small feat. Malek Bennabi and Muhammad al-Tahir ibn Ashur are the strength of Muslim thought and its modern symbols. That is what made them Renaissance heroes.

Neither these nor the movements they created were the end of the Renaissance. It is an epochal link in the process of Tajdidi -Renaissance- which has been happening continuously throughout history. Tajdeed is the possibility that makes Islam fit for constant innovation. The gates of this possibility will remain open until the end of time. It is the process of Tajdeed that makes Islam timeless, interacts and co-exists with the present. It is through constant growth and evolution that the Islamic experience has developed in the world. This is the first lesson to be learned from the history of Islam. Cut off from the flow and link of this long history, Muslims will become mere mobs.

Prophets are our role models. Ultimately, they were human liberators. Prophets freed their people from the forces of evil and oppression and cleansed them from all wrong tendencies that were influencing their lives. These trends had religious, social, economic and political dimensions. The diversity of times, countries and situations also had an impact on the preaching of the prophets. They called for a complete change. They are our first reference in the journey of revival. This is the meaning of the Qur'anic verse, 'Follow their way' (al-An'am 90).

In Indian Context

Islamic revivalism performed a historic task in the Indian social environment. Sir Sayed Ahmad Khan, Justice Amir Ali and Abul Kalam Azad led the torch in India. The situation in the country today is not the same as it was during its formation. The Muslim community and the Indian community are going through a completely different and complex situation. We can distinguish four phases during which the Islamic movement took shape and developed in India:

One, colonial period: This is the phase of Islam's anti-imperialist resistance. It was the collapse of Muslim Spain that paved the way for the voyages of Vasco da Gama and Columbus, which marked the beginning of Western colonialism. Columbus began his journey of conquest in 1492 when Granada, the last Muslim city in Spain, fell to the enemy. The colonization started by the Spanish emperor King Ferdinand and Queen Isabella with the blessing of the then Catholic Church hurt Muslims politically and religiously.

Naturally, this led Muslim scholars, leaders, movements and associations to the anti-colonial struggle. In 1919, Germany lost World War I. Britain and France, who were allies, won. This provided an opportunity for Britain to intervene politically in Turkey, which was on the side of Germany. They abolished the

Ottoman Caliphate. Fifteen countries, including Saudi Arabia, Jordan, Syria, Palestine, Egypt, Iran, Iraq, Kuwait, Algeria, Sudan, Libya, Chechnya, Bosnia, and Kosovo, which were under the control of the Caliphate, became Western colonies or were subjected to colonial political intervention.

The collapse of the Ottoman Empire in Turkey played a crucial role in shaping the Islamic Renaissance of the 20th century. Syria, Palestine, Egypt, Iran, Iraq, Kuwait, Algeria, Sudan, Libya, Chechnya, Bosnia, Kosovo, and fifteen other countries became Western colonies or were subject to political intervention. The interventions of the Muslim community were prominent at all important milestones in the history of anti-colonial struggles in the Indian subcontinent. To some extent, the Muslim masses and scholars had entered the leadership position of the freedom struggle. The Ulama of Darul Uloom Deoband played a leading role in the First Freedom Movement of 1857.

India and the Muslims of that time were crucial in determining the priorities of the Islamic movement. Had it not been for partition, Muslims would have been the dominant social group in the Indian subcontinent. It is the same It encouraged the colonial powers to reinforce Muslim-Hindu polarization, adopt a policy of divide and rule, and ultimately lead to India-Pakistan partition. This is the first stage that the Islamic movement in India has passed.

The second stage: is the transition period. This phase was complex and fraught with tension, both for India and for Muslims. A large population and territory became three nations. Muslims were the largest community in India that suffered the brunt of the impact and backlash of Partition. Partition left the community orphaned and leaderless. Insecurity haunted Muslims. The Islamic movement, though to a lesser extent, also found it difficult to overcome the problems of division. The top-tier leaders had mostly become part of Pakistan. This has created great difficulties in formulating the policy and programs of the movement.

The third phase: is the postmodern period. This was a time when capitalism and socialism, which the Islamic movement rejected ideologically, failed in practice and democracy and secularism constantly demonstrated their inherent weaknesses. As all units of the social hierarchy (individual, family, society, nation) constantly faced its impact, the movement tried to confront it with the tools immediately ahead. As a renaissance movement, it can be examined whether the conceptual clarity that revival movements possessed at the time of its formation was possible at this stage of its implementation.

Overdue Islamic Revivalism

The fourth step: is the situation we are facing currently. Globally the current situation is called the 'post-truth era'. This trend is called 'post-truth' because emotion, personal beliefs and prejudices influence more than facts in forming a public opinion. Islamophobia is spreading worldwide. Indian nationalism becomes communal nationalism. Islam is perceived by many as a religion outside the compatibility of secularism. A terrible situation has gripped the country where Muslims are attacked or killed for the sole reason of being religious. It may seem quite unusual, but it is also a time when abnormalities become natural. Social scientists call this period the post-normal time. Violent communalism fascism is at its most violent phase. Corporatism has taken hold of governance by inventing new methods of exploitation.

We must categorize the problems we face and determine those that require immediate attention. In this, we also have the model of the prophets. The mujtahids - researchers - Imams have also given us such examples. The commission of the prophets was complicated by many thorny issues. They did not approach and consider all issues in the same measure and level. They problematized something by setting priorities. It became their subject of instruction. We should not fail to understand that it was part of God's plan.

Dawat in Islam is not mere propaganda. Prayer plays a crucial role in the process of social reconstruction. It is the exchange of ideas and dedication to practice necessary for the reform and liberation of the individual and society. Reform and emancipation were the mission of the prophets. Both served as complements. The activities of the Prophets can thus be divided into two: First, Da'wat. Two, Jihad. While da'wah is purely conceptual and discursive, jihad is ideological and political. While da'wah focuses on the liberation of the individual, the goal of Jihad is social liberation. Da'wah and Jihad also build a society in its faith, ideals and cultural identity and enable it to undertake the task of emancipation of all mankind. In contemporary India, Islamic Jihad is inapplicable as it is abhorrent to the Indian constitutional ethos of secularism, democracy and pluralism. Da'wa with false allures is against Islam as it gives primacy to personal intellect and discretion.

But Da'wah, practised all over the world today, especially in areas where traditional Muslim thought and society prevail, is aimed solely at the individual's ascension to heaven. His social status, prestige, the problems he faces politically and economically and their solution have not grown into the subject of Da'wat. The Islamic renaissance of the twentieth century succeeded in highlighting the integrity of Islam. It made possible its political and social expression. But it remains to be seen whether the revivalist movements, especially in India, have been able to develop and establish the efficient expression of preaching. The processes of Ijtihad and jihad are the organic capacity of Islam to move with the times. Ijtihad will illuminate the theoretical and conceptual core of Islam and will enable its application. These determine the content, style and priority of the da'wah.

Unfortunately, in post-partition India, Da'wat has been reduced to a separate form of religious propaganda from ijtihad and revival into concerted conversion and mad Jihad. Da'wat has two parts: First: ideal. In the technical language of Islam, this is what Aqeedah is about. Aqeedah can be divided into three parts namely Tawheed, Risalat and Akhirat. These are the basis (asl) of Islam and da'wah. The Prophets spoke first of all about Allah, the angels, the scriptures, the prophets and the hereafter. The main part of Da'wat is its content and language. From the foundation of the ideal, the first part, the problems faced by the people determine the content of the prayer. Note the Qur'anic verse, 'We have not sent a prophet except in the language of the people' (Ibrahim 4). Here the Arabic expression 'Lisaan al-Qoum', meaning the language of the people, refers not only to the spoken language. Lisanul Qaum also includes the concept of one who speaks about the people and their problems. Thus, all the Prophets spoke about their people, the problems they faced and their solutions. So Da'wat is both ideal and practice. Understanding problems and solving them. But today's Da'wah has been reduced to incomplete religious propaganda.

There are three reasons for this: First, the narrow view propagated by the West that Muslims and non-Muslims still hold to some extent about religion. The second reason is the influence of Salafi and Tablighi ideology which purported to reduce Islam into scriptures and social alienation. Third, the influence of the radical Islamist school of thought pushes religion and life into two incompatible poles. Spiritual Islam and cultural Islam must be universally accepted and political Islam rejected to push forward Islamic revivalist agendas. The Islamic movement must face the question of what the strategy is to overcome this with courage.

CHAPTER XIV

Muslim Personal Law In The Constituent Assembly: A Historical And Legal Perspective

The formation of the Indian Constitution was a monumental event that sought to unify a deeply diverse and complex society. One of the most contentious issues debated during the Constituent Assembly's deliberations was the question of personal laws, particularly Muslim Personal Law. The discussions around this topic revealed deep-seated tensions between the desire to create a uniform legal framework for all citizens and the need to respect the religious and cultural diversity of India's people.

Muslim Personal Law, which governs matters of marriage, divorce, inheritance, and other family-related issues among Muslims in India, has its roots in Islamic jurisprudence. The Constituent Assembly debates on this subject were marked by a struggle to balance the secular ideals enshrined in the Constitution with the protection of religious freedoms. This essay delves into the historical context, the debates within the Constituent Assembly, and the implications of the decisions made regarding Muslim Personal Law, highlighting the complexities and challenges that continue to shape this area of law in India.

Before delving into the Constituent Assembly debates, it is essential to understand the historical context of Muslim Personal Law in India. During the British colonial period, the British administration adopted a policy of non-interference in religious matters, particularly in personal laws. This approach was intended to maintain social order and avoid conflicts with religious communities.

Muslim Personal Law was codified to a certain extent with the enactment of the Shariat Act of 1937, which aimed to ensure that

Muslims in India were governed by Islamic law in personal matters, rather than customary practices that had developed over time. The Act reinforced the application of Sharia law in matters of marriage, divorce, inheritance, and other family-related issues, while leaving certain areas like criminal law under the jurisdiction of secular, British-imposed laws.

The British policy of preserving religious personal laws was driven by pragmatic considerations, as it allowed the colonial administration to govern a diverse population with minimal resistance. However, this policy also sowed the seeds of future conflicts, as it institutionalized legal pluralism and created distinct legal frameworks for different religious communities.

The Constituent Assembly And The Challenge Of Personal Laws

When the Constituent Assembly of India began its deliberations in December 1946, the issue of personal laws quickly emerged as a major point of contention. The Assembly was tasked with drafting a Constitution that would govern a newly independent India, a country characterized by its vast cultural, religious, and linguistic diversity. The framers of the Constitution faced the difficult task of reconciling the principles of secularism and individual rights with the need to respect religious and cultural traditions.

One of the key questions debated in the Assembly was whether India should have a Uniform Civil Code (UCC) that would apply to all citizens, regardless of their religion, or whether personal laws should be preserved for different religious communities. The debate was not merely a legal one; it was deeply intertwined with issues of identity, autonomy, and the role of religion in the public sphere.

Debates On Muslim Personal Law In The Constituent Assembly

The debates on Muslim Personal Law in the Constituent Assembly were marked by sharp differences of opinion among the members. These debates centered on several key issues: the role of the state in regulating personal laws, the implications of a Uniform

Civil Code, and the protection of minority rights.

1. The Role of the State in Regulating Personal Laws

One of the central issues in the debate was the extent to which the state should intervene in the regulation of personal laws. Some members of the Assembly, such as B.R. Ambedkar, the Chairman of the Drafting Committee, argued that the state had a duty to enact laws that would promote social reform and protect individual rights, even if it meant challenging religious traditions. Ambedkar was a strong advocate for a Uniform Civil Code, which he believed would help eliminate gender discrimination and promote social justice.

On the other hand, many Muslim members of the Assembly, including leaders like Maulana Hasrat Mohani and Naziruddin Ahmad, argued that Muslim Personal Law was an integral part of their religious identity and should be preserved. They contended that any attempt to impose a Uniform Civil Code would be seen as an infringement on their religious freedoms and could lead to social unrest. They emphasized that Islamic law was divinely ordained and that any changes to it should come from within the community, rather than being imposed by the state.

2. The Uniform Civil Code: A Contentious Proposal

The proposal for a Uniform Civil Code was one of the most contentious issues debated in the Constituent Assembly. Proponents of the UCC, including Ambedkar and K.M. Munshi, argued that a common set of laws governing all citizens was essential for achieving national unity and promoting gender equality. They contended that personal laws based on religion were inherently discriminatory, particularly against women, and that a UCC would help create a more just and egalitarian society.

Opponents of the UCC, however, viewed it as a threat to the religious and cultural autonomy of minority communities. Muslim members of the Assembly were particularly vocal in their opposition, arguing that the imposition of a UCC would violate their right to religious freedom, which was guaranteed under the Constitution. They feared that a UCC would undermine the distinct identity of the Muslim community and erode the protections provided by Muslim Personal Law.

The debates on the UCC also highlighted broader concerns about the relationship between religion and the state in a secular India. Some members of the Assembly, such as H.V. Kamath, argued that the state should adopt a hands-off approach to religious matters and allow communities to govern themselves according to their own traditions. Others, like Ambedkar, believed that the state had a responsibility to intervene in matters of social justice, even if it meant challenging religious norms.

3. Protection of Minority Rights

The protection of minority rights was a central concern for many members of the Constituent Assembly, particularly in the context of the ongoing communal tensions following the Partition of India. Muslim members of the Assembly were particularly concerned about the protection of their personal laws, which they saw as a crucial aspect of their religious and cultural identity.

The debates on Muslim Personal Law were deeply influenced by the broader context of minority rights in post-Partition India. The experience of Partition, which had been accompanied by widespread violence and displacement, had heightened the sense of insecurity among religious minorities, particularly Muslims. Many Muslim members of the Assembly feared that the imposition of a UCC would further marginalize their community and erode their religious rights.

In response to these concerns, the Constituent Assembly ultimately decided to include provisions in the Constitution that would protect the rights of religious minorities, including their right to be governed by their own personal laws. Article 25 of the Constitution guarantees the freedom of religion, while Article 26 allows religious communities to manage their own affairs in matters of religion. These provisions were seen as essential for preserving the cultural and religious diversity of India.

The Compromise: Article 44 And The Directive Principles Of State Policy

The debates on Muslim Personal Law and the Uniform Civil Code ultimately resulted in a compromise that was reflected in the final text of the Constitution. While the Constitution guarantees the right to religious freedom and the protection of personal laws, it also includes a provision for a Uniform Civil Code in the Directive Principles of State Policy.

Article 44 of the Constitution states: "The State shall endeavor to secure for the citizens a uniform civil code throughout the territory of India." However, unlike the fundamental rights, which are justiciable and enforceable by the courts, the Directive Principles are non-justiciable, meaning that they are not legally enforceable but are intended to guide the government in making laws and policies.

The inclusion of Article 44 was a reflection of the Constituent Assembly's desire to eventually move towards a more uniform legal framework, while also recognizing the need to protect religious freedoms in the present. It was seen as a compromise that would allow for gradual social reform, rather than imposing a UCC immediately.

This compromise was not without its critics. Some members of the Assembly, including Ambedkar, were disappointed that the UCC was relegated to the Directive Principles, rather than being made a justiciable right. However, others saw it as a pragmatic solution that would allow for the protection of minority rights while also laying the groundwork for future reforms.

The Impact Of The Constituent Assembly Debates On Muslim Personal Law

The debates on Muslim Personal Law in the Constituent Assembly had a profound impact on the legal and social landscape of post-independence India. The decisions made during these debates have continued to shape the relationship between law, religion, and the state in India.

1. Preservation of Legal Pluralism

One of the most significant outcomes of the Constituent Assembly debates was the preservation of legal pluralism in India.

The decision to allow religious communities to be governed by their own personal laws has meant that India continues to have multiple legal systems coexisting side by side. While this has allowed for the protection of religious and cultural diversity, it has also led to ongoing debates about the implications of legal pluralism for gender justice and social equality.

2. Ongoing Debates on the Uniform Civil Code

The inclusion of Article 44 in the Directive Principles of State Policy has kept the debate on the Uniform Civil Code alive in India. While successive governments have taken steps towards legal reform in areas such as marriage and divorce, the UCC remains a contentious issue. The debate continues to be characterized by tensions between the goals of national unity and gender equality, on the one hand, and the protection of religious freedoms and minority rights, on the other.

The Shah Bano case in 1985 and the subsequent enactment of the Muslim Women (Protection of Rights on Divorce) Act in 1986 brought the issue of the UCC back into the national spotlight, highlighting the challenges of implementing a common legal framework in a religiously diverse society

CHAPTER XV

The Shah Bano Case Controversy And Popular Debates On Muslim Personal Law

The Shah Bano case, a landmark judgment in Indian legal history, has been a subject of intense controversy and debate since the 1980s. It not only raised significant questions about the interplay between law and religion in India but also brought to the fore the complexities of gender justice, secularism, and minority rights in a pluralistic society. The case revolved around a simple issue of maintenance for a divorced Muslim woman, yet it ignited a national debate that resonated with the larger questions of the Uniform Civil Code (UCC), the role of religious personal laws, and the protection of women's rights in India.

This essay delves into the Shah Bano case, exploring the legal and socio-political dimensions of the controversy it sparked, and analyzing its profound impact on Indian society. The case is often cited as a turning point in the discourse on secularism and the rights of minorities in India, and it continues to influence debates on personal laws and gender justice to this day.

The Background Of The Shah Bano Case

The Shah Bano case arose in 1978 when a 62-year-old Muslim woman, Shah Bano Begum, filed a petition in the Supreme Court of India seeking maintenance from her husband, Mohammed Ahmed Khan, who had divorced her through triple talaq. Shah Bano had been married for over four decades and had five children. After her husband unilaterally divorced her, he stopped providing for her maintenance, which left her destitute.

Under the Indian legal framework, Section 125 of the Criminal Procedure Code (CrPC) entitles a wife to seek maintenance from her husband if she is unable to support herself. Shah Bano invoked this provision to claim maintenance, even though Islamic law, as practiced in India, did not traditionally recognize a divorced woman's right to maintenance beyond the iddat period (a period of three months following the divorce).

The local court initially ruled in Shah Bano's favor, ordering her husband to pay her a monthly maintenance amount. Dissatisfied with this decision, Ahmed Khan appealed to the Supreme Court, arguing that since both he and Shah Bano were Muslims, the case should be governed by Muslim Personal Law, which does not mandate maintenance beyond the iddat period. The case thus brought to the forefront the conflict between a secular legal provision and religious personal laws.

The Supreme Court Judgment

In 1985, the Supreme Court of India delivered its judgment in the Shah Bano case, which became a watershed moment in Indian legal history. The court upheld Shah Bano's right to maintenance under Section 125 of the CrPC, ruling that this provision applies to all citizens regardless of their religion. The judgment stated that the CrPC was a secular law that overruled religious personal laws in matters of maintenance and that a divorced woman, regardless of her religion, was entitled to maintenance from her ex-husband if she could not support herself.

Justice Y.V. Chandrachud, who authored the judgment, emphasized that the application of a common civil code as envisioned in Article 44 of the Indian Constitution would help secure justice for all citizens, particularly women. The judgment also critiqued the discriminatory aspects of Muslim Personal Law, particularly its treatment of women in matters of divorce and maintenance. The court's decision was hailed by many as a victory for women's rights and a step towards gender equality.

However, the judgment also sparked a significant backlash from conservative sections of the Muslim community, who viewed it as an infringement on their religious rights and an attack on the sanctity of Muslim Personal Law. The judgment was seen as a challenge to the autonomy of religious communities to govern their personal matters according to their own laws, and it led to a nationwide debate on the role of secularism and the state's intervention in religious affairs.

The Political And Social Backlash

The Shah Bano case quickly became a flashpoint for communal tensions in India. The Supreme Court's judgment was perceived by many Muslims as an encroachment on their religious freedoms, guaranteed under Articles 25 to 28 of the Indian Constitution. Islamic religious leaders and conservative organizations vehemently opposed the judgment, arguing that it violated the principles of Shariat and threatened the religious identity of the Muslim community.

The controversy gained political traction, with Muslim leaders organizing mass protests and demonstrations across the country. They argued that the judgment was an imposition of a secular law on a religious community and that it undermined the authority of Muslim Personal Law. The All India Muslim Personal Law Board (AIMPLB) played a central role in mobilizing opposition to the judgment, framing it as an existential threat to the community's religious autonomy.

Amidst growing pressure from the Muslim community, the then Prime Minister Rajiv Gandhi's government found itself in a difficult position. The government was concerned about the potential for communal unrest and sought to pacify the Muslim community by taking legislative action. In 1986, the government passed the Muslim Women (Protection of Rights on Divorce) Act, which effectively overturned the Supreme Court's judgment in the Shah Bano case. The Act limited the husband's liability to provide maintenance to the iddat period and allowed Muslim women to seek maintenance only from their relatives or through the Waqf Board if they were unable to support themselves.

The passage of the Muslim Women Act was widely criticized by women's rights groups, secular organizations, and political opponents of the Congress party. Critics argued that the Act was a regressive measure that reinforced gender discrimination within the Muslim community and undermined the principle of equality before the law. They contended that the government had caved to religious pressure and sacrificed the rights of Muslim women in the name of appeasement politics.

The Debate On Secularism And Minority Rights

The Shah Bano case and the subsequent passage of the Muslim Women Act reignited a broader debate on secularism and minority rights in India. The controversy highlighted the tension between the state's commitment to secularism and its obligation to protect the rights of religious minorities. On one hand, the state's intervention in the Shah Bano case was seen as a necessary step to uphold the principles of gender justice and equality. On the other hand, the backlash against the judgment and the enactment of the Muslim Women Act underscored the challenges of enforcing secular laws in a religiously diverse society.

The case also raised important questions about the nature of secularism in India. Unlike the Western model of secularism, which advocates a strict separation of religion and state, Indian secularism is characterized by the principle of "sarva dharma samabhava" (equal respect for all religions). This model allows the state to engage with religious communities and accommodate their personal laws, while also striving to uphold the constitutional values of equality and justice.

The Shah Bano controversy exposed the limitations of this model of secularism, particularly in its ability to balance the competing demands of religious freedom and gender justice. It highlighted the need for a more nuanced approach to secularism, one that respects religious diversity while also ensuring that the fundamental rights of all citizens, especially women, are protected.

The case also brought to the forefront the issue of the Uniform Civil Code (UCC), which has been a long-standing demand of those who advocate for a common set of laws governing all citizens, regardless of their religion. The Shah Bano judgment was seen by many as a call for the implementation of a UCC, which would eliminate the disparities between different personal laws and provide equal protection to all citizens. However, the strong opposition to the judgment from the Muslim community underscored the challenges of achieving consensus on such a sensitive issue.

Impact On Indian Society

The Shah Bano case had a profound and lasting impact on Indian society, influencing debates on personal laws, gender justice, and the rights of religious minorities. One of the most significant impacts was the increased visibility of women's rights issues within the Muslim community. The case brought to light the challenges faced by Muslim women under the existing personal law system and sparked a broader movement for reform within the community.

Women's rights activists and organizations seized the opportunity to advocate for greater legal protections for Muslim women, including the right to maintenance, divorce, and inheritance. The controversy also led to the formation of new women's organizations, such as the Bharatiya Muslim Mahila Andolan (BMMA), which have been at the forefront of the struggle for gender justice within the Muslim community.

The case also had a significant impact on the political landscape in India. The Congress party's decision to pass the Muslim Women Act was widely criticized as an act of "minority appeasement," and it alienated many of its traditional supporters. The backlash against the Act contributed to the rise of the Bharatiya Janata Party (BJP), which positioned itself as a champion of a Uniform Civil Code and secularism. The BJP's emphasis on a UCC became a key element of its political platform, and it has continued to advocate for the implementation of a UCC as a means of ensuring equal rights for all citizens.

The Shah Bano case also had implications for the broader debate on the relationship between religion and the state in India. The controversy underscored the challenges of governing a religiously diverse society and highlighted the need for a more inclusive and pluralistic approach to secularism. It also raised important questions about the role of the judiciary in interpreting and enforcing personal laws, and the extent to which the state should intervene in matters of religious law.

In the years following the Shah Bano case, there have been several attempts to reform Muslim Personal Law, particularly in the areas of divorce and maintenance. In 2017, the Supreme Court of India delivered another landmark judgment in the case of Shayara Bano v. Union of India, in which it declared the practice of triple talaq to be unconstitutional. This judgment was seen as a continuation of the struggle for gender justice that began with the Shah Bano case, and it has further fueled the debate on the need for a Uniform Civil Code.

CHAPTER XVI

The Uniform Civil Code Debate In India: A Focus On Muslim Personal Law

The Uniform Civil Code (UCC) has been a subject of intense debate in India, embodying the tension between individual rights, religious freedom, and the vision of a unified legal framework for the nation. The proposal to establish a UCC, which would replace the personal laws of various religious communities with a common set of laws governing marriage, divorce, inheritance, and adoption, has sparked controversy, particularly within the Muslim community. Muslim Personal Law, derived from the Shariat (Islamic law), is deeply intertwined with religious identity and practice, making the prospect of a UCC a contentious issue. This essay seeks to explore the historical context, constitutional provisions, and the arguments surrounding the UCC, with a special focus on the implications for Muslim Personal Law in India.

Historical Background Of The Uniform Civil Code

The debate over the UCC in India is not a recent phenomenon; it has its roots in the colonial period when the British administration first codified laws for different religious communities. The British policy of non-interference in religious affairs led to the formalization of Hindu and Muslim personal laws, with the latter being governed largely by the Shariat. This policy of maintaining separate personal laws for different communities was based on the belief that such laws were integral to religious identity and autonomy.

After India gained independence in 1947, the issue of a UCC became a focal point during the drafting of the Indian Constitution. The framers of the Constitution were divided on the matter, with some advocating for a UCC as a means to promote national unity and social reform, while others emphasized the need to respect the cultural and religious diversity of the country. Ultimately, Article 44 of the Directive Principles of State Policy was included in the Constitution, stating that "The State shall endeavor to secure for the citizens a uniform civil code throughout the territory of India." However, this provision was non-binding, and the implementation of a UCC was left to the discretion of the state, resulting in a prolonged and ongoing debate.

Constitutional Provisions And The Uniform Civil Code

The Indian Constitution embodies a delicate balance between the principles of secularism, religious freedom, and the pursuit of social justice. Article 44 of the Directive Principles of State Policy reflects the vision of the framers for a common civil code, but its non-justiciable nature has led to its relegation to the realm of ideals rather than enforceable rights. The fundamental rights enshrined in Articles 25 to 28 guarantee religious freedom, allowing communities to govern their personal matters according to their religious laws.

This constitutional framework has led to a situation where multiple personal laws coexist, each governing marriage, divorce, inheritance, and adoption according to religious traditions. For the Muslim community, these matters are governed by the Shariat, which is seen as a divine and immutable law. The tension between the Directive Principles and the fundamental rights has been a central theme in the UCC debate, raising questions about the nature of secularism in India and the feasibility of implementing a common civil code.

The judiciary has played a significant role in the UCC debate, often highlighting the need for a common civil code while acknowledging the complexities of enforcing such a code in a pluralistic society. Landmark cases like Shah Bano (1985) and Sarla Mudgal (1995) have brought the issue of the UCC to the forefront, with the courts calling for legislative action to implement a UCC. However, these calls have often been met with resistance from various religious communities, particularly Muslims, who view such moves as an infringement on their religious rights.

Muslim Personal Law: An Overview

Muslim Personal Law in India is primarily derived from the Shariat, which governs various aspects of personal life, including marriage, divorce, inheritance, and maintenance. The Shariat Application Act of 1937 formalized the application of Islamic law to Muslims in matters of personal law, reinforcing the community's autonomy in these areas. This act was seen as a way to protect the religious identity of Muslims in a predominantly Hindu society, and it has remained largely unchanged since its enactment.

Key features of Muslim Personal Law include the concepts of "nikah" (marriage) and "talaq" (divorce), which are central to the regulation of family life. Islamic inheritance laws, based on the principles of the Quran and Hadith, provide specific rules for the distribution of property, with a focus on male heirs but also including provisions for the rights of female relatives. Maintenance and custody are also governed by Islamic principles, although these have been subject to legal scrutiny and debate, particularly in cases like Shah Bano, where the Supreme Court called for reforms to address issues of gender justice.

Despite its religious foundation, Muslim Personal Law has been a subject of debate within the community, with calls for reforms to address issues related to gender justice and modernization. However, these debates are often overshadowed by concerns about maintaining religious identity and autonomy, leading to resistance against any attempts to reform Muslim Personal Law from outside the community.

Arguments For And Against A Uniform Civil Code

The debate over the UCC is characterized by a wide range of arguments, both in favor of and against its implementation. Proponents of the UCC argue that it is essential for ensuring equality before the law, particularly in terms of gender justice. They contend that personal laws, especially those governing Muslims, often discriminate against women, and a UCC would provide equal rights to all citizens, regardless of their religion.

From a legal perspective, advocates of the UCC emphasize the need for uniformity in the legal system. They argue that the coexistence of multiple personal laws creates confusion and inequality, and a UCC would streamline legal processes and enhance justice. Additionally, a UCC is seen as a means of promoting national integration by fostering a sense of unity among citizens and reducing communal tensions.

On the other hand, opponents of the UCC argue that it would infringe upon religious freedom and undermine the cultural diversity that defines India. They believe that personal laws are an expression of religious identity and should be preserved in a pluralistic society. For the Muslim community, the UCC is often seen as a threat to their religious autonomy and a potential imposition of majoritarian values.

Critics of the UCC also point to the practical challenges of implementing such a code in a diverse country like India. The vast differences in cultural practices, legal traditions, and social norms across communities make it difficult to create a one-size-fits-all legal framework. They argue that any attempt to impose a UCC could lead to increased social unrest and further polarization along religious lines.

Impact Of A Uniform Civil Code On Muslim Personal Law

If a UCC were to be implemented, it would have significant implications for Muslim Personal Law. The most immediate impact would be on marriage and divorce laws, where the UCC could standardize practices and potentially override Islamic practices like "triple talaq" and "halala." This could lead to legal conflicts between the state and the community, as well as resistance from those who view these practices as integral to their religious identity.

Islamic inheritance laws, which are currently protected under Muslim Personal Law, might also be replaced by a common set of rules that do not account for the specificities of Shariah law. This could create tensions within the community, particularly among those who believe that Islamic inheritance laws are divinely ordained and should not be altered by human intervention.

The UCC could also bring uniformity to maintenance and custody laws, potentially providing greater protection for women but also challenging the traditional norms upheld by Muslim Personal Law. This could lead to a re-examination of the balance between gender justice and religious rights, with implications for the broader debate on secularism and social reform in India.

Beyond the legal changes, the implementation of a UCC would have far-reaching socio-political implications for the Muslim community. Many Muslims may perceive the UCC as an attack on their religious identity and autonomy, leading to increased resistance and social unrest. The community may view the UCC as an attempt to dilute their religious practices and impose majoritarian values, further deepening the divide between religious communities in India.

The UCC debate also highlights the tension between gender justice and religious rights. While the UCC could enhance gender equality by providing uniform legal protections, it could also be seen as disregarding the religious rights of Muslim women who wish to follow their personal laws. This tension is emblematic of the broader challenges facing India as it seeks to balance the principles of secularism, religious freedom, and social justice in a diverse and pluralistic society.

Case Studies And Comparative Perspectives

To better understand the implications of a UCC on Muslim Personal Law, it is helpful to examine case studies and comparative perspectives. The Shah Bano case (1985) is one of the most significant legal battles in this context. Shah Bano, a Muslim woman, was denied maintenance by her husband after divorce, leading her to seek legal redress under Section 125 of the Criminal Procedure Code. The Supreme Court ruled in her favor, stating that she was entitled to maintenance. This judgment sparked widespread controversy, leading to the enactment of the Muslim Women (Protection of Rights on Divorce) Act, 1986, which limited the applicability of the Supreme Court's ruling and reaffirmed the primacy of Muslim Personal Law in matters of divorce and maintenance.

The Shah Bano case is often cited as a turning point in the UCC debate, highlighting the complexities of balancing gender justice with religious rights. The case also underscored the political dimensions of the UCC debate, as the government's response to the Supreme Court's ruling was seen by many as an attempt to placate conservative elements within the Muslim community.

Comparative perspectives from other countries can also provide valuable insights into the UCC debate in India. For example, several Muslim-majority countries, such as Turkey and Tunisia, have implemented reforms to their personal laws, incorporating elements of a civil code while retaining certain aspects of Sharia.

CHAPTER XVII

The Dilemma Od Waqf

The institution of Waqf, an Islamic endowment for religious, educational, or charitable purposes, has played a significant role in the socio-economic and religious life of Muslims in India. Waqf properties have historically been used to fund mosques, schools, orphanages, and other public welfare institutions, making them a crucial element of the community's infrastructure. However, the regulation and management of Waqf properties have been fraught with challenges, particularly during and after the colonial period in India.

This essay examines the evolution of Waqf regulation in India, focusing on the colonial and post-independence periods. It explores the legal and administrative frameworks that have governed Waqf properties, the impact of colonial policies, and the efforts made by independent India to reform and regulate Waqf management. By tracing the historical trajectory of Waqf regulation, this essay aims to provide a comprehensive understanding of the complexities and challenges associated with this important institution.

The Concept Of Waqf: Origins And Significance

Before delving into the regulatory aspects, it is important to understand the concept of Waqf and its significance in Islamic law. The term "Waqf" is derived from the Arabic root "waqafa," which means to stop, contain, or preserve. In Islamic jurisprudence, a Waqf refers to a permanent dedication of property, either movable or immovable, for religious, pious, or charitable purposes. Once a property is dedicated as Waqf, it becomes inalienable and cannot be sold, inherited, or otherwise disposed of.

The institution of Waqf has its origins in early Islamic history, with the Prophet Muhammad himself establishing the first Waqf in the form of a well in Medina for public use. Over time, the practice of creating Waqfs became widespread across the Islamic world, serving as a means of supporting religious institutions, education, healthcare, and other forms of social welfare.

In India, the Waqf system was introduced by Muslim rulers during the medieval period, and it flourished under the Mughal Empire. The Mughal rulers, as well as wealthy individuals, established numerous Waqfs to fund mosques, madrasas (Islamic schools), and other charitable institutions. These Waqfs played a vital role in sustaining the religious and cultural life of the Muslim community.

Waqf Regulation During The Colonial Period

The advent of British colonial rule in India marked a significant turning point in the regulation and management of Waqf properties. The British administration's approach to Waqf was shaped by its broader policy of legal reform and the need to establish control over religious and charitable endowments. The colonial period saw the introduction of new legal frameworks that had a profound impact on the traditional Waqf system.

1. Early Colonial Policies and Legal Reforms

In the early years of British rule, the colonial administration largely adhered to a policy of non-interference in religious matters, including Waqf. However, as the British consolidated their control over India, they began to introduce legal reforms that affected Waqf management. One of the earliest measures was the Bengal Regulation XIX of 1810, which was primarily aimed at curbing the mismanagement of religious endowments, including Waqf properties. The regulation empowered the colonial government to take over the management of endowments that were being misused or neglected.

The British administration's interest in regulating Waqf was also driven by financial considerations. Waqf properties, being inalienable, were exempt from taxes, which led to a loss of revenue for the colonial government. To address this, the British introduced the Bengal Waqf Act of 1863, which sought to bring Waqf properties under greater government supervision. The Act provided for the appointment of government officials to oversee the management of Waqf properties and ensure that they were used for their intended purposes.

2. The Wakf Validating Act of 1913

The most significant legal development in the regulation of Waqf during the colonial period was the enactment of the Wakf Validating Act of 1913. The Act was a response to a series of legal challenges to the validity of Waqfs, particularly those created for the benefit of the settlor's family (known as Waqf-alal-aulad). In several court cases, British judges had ruled that such Waqfs were invalid under Islamic law, leading to widespread concern among the Muslim community.

The Wakf Validating Act of 1913 sought to address these concerns by recognizing the validity of Waqf-alal-aulad and affirming the legality of family Waqfs. The Act was seen as a significant victory for the Muslim community, as it protected the institution of Waqf from further legal challenges and ensured that Waqf properties could continue to be used for religious and charitable purposes.

However, the Act also had its limitations. While it provided legal recognition to Waqfs, it did not address the issue of mismanagement or the lack of proper regulation. As a result, many Waqf properties continued to suffer from neglect, corruption, and encroachments, leading to a decline in their effectiveness as instruments of social welfare.

3. The Role of the Muslim Community

Throughout the colonial period, the Muslim community played an active role in advocating for the protection and regulation of Waqf properties. Muslim leaders and organizations, such as the All India Muslim League, lobbied the British government to enact laws that would safeguard Waqf properties and ensure their proper management. They also sought to create awareness within the community about the importance of Waqf and the need to prevent its misuse.

In addition to legal advocacy, the Muslim community also established various Waqf boards and committees to oversee the management of Waqf properties. These boards were responsible for maintaining records, auditing accounts, and ensuring that Waqf properties were used in accordance with Islamic principles. However, the effectiveness of these boards varied, and many Waqf properties continued to face challenges related to mismanagement and encroachments.

Waqf Regulation In Post-Independence India

The regulation of Waqf properties remained a significant issue in post-independence India. The newly independent nation faced the challenge of balancing the need for effective regulation with the protection of religious freedoms guaranteed by the Constitution. The government of India undertook several legislative and administrative measures to reform and regulate the management of Waqf properties, with varying degrees of success.

1. The Wakf Act of 1954

One of the first major legislative measures undertaken by the Indian government to regulate Waqf properties was the Wakf Act of 1954. The Act was enacted with the aim of providing a comprehensive legal framework for the management and administration of Waqf properties across the country. It sought to address the issues of mismanagement, corruption, and encroachments that had plagued Waqf properties during the colonial period.

The Wakf Act of 1954 established Central and State Wakf Boards, which were tasked with the responsibility of overseeing the management of Waqf properties. These boards were empowered to maintain records of Waqf properties, conduct surveys, and take legal action against those who misused or encroached upon Waqf land. The Act also provided for the appointment of Mutawallis (Waqf managers) and laid down rules for their conduct and responsibilities.

While the Wakf Act of 1954 was a significant step forward in the regulation of Waqf properties, its implementation faced several challenges. The lack of adequate resources, poor enforcement, and bureaucratic inefficiencies hindered the effectiveness of the Wakf

Boards. Additionally, the Act did not fully address the issue of encroachments, which continued to be a major problem for Waqf properties.

2. The Wakf (Amendment) Act of 1995

In response to the continuing challenges in the regulation of Waqf properties, the Indian government enacted the Wakf (Amendment) Act of 1995. The Amendment Act sought to strengthen the existing legal framework and improve the management and administration of Waqf properties.

The Wakf (Amendment) Act of 1995 introduced several important changes, including stricter provisions for the removal of encroachments on Waqf properties, greater transparency in the functioning of Wakf Boards, and enhanced powers for the boards to take legal action against errant Mutawallis. The Amendment Act also mandated regular surveys of Waqf properties and the maintenance of updated records.

The 1995 Amendment Act was seen as a significant improvement over the earlier legislation, as it addressed some of the key issues that had plagued Waqf regulation in India. However, the implementation of the Act continued to face challenges, particularly in terms of enforcement and the availability of resources.

3. The Sachar Committee Report and Its Impact

The issue of Waqf regulation gained renewed attention in the early 2000s with the publication of the Sachar Committee Report in 2006. The Sachar Committee, which was tasked with assessing the socio-economic status of Muslims in India, highlighted the critical role of Waqf properties in the welfare of the Muslim community and the need for effective regulation.

The Sachar Committee Report identified several issues related to Waqf properties, including widespread encroachments, mismanagement, and the underutilization of Waqf assets. The report estimated that the total value of Waqf properties in India was worth billions of rupees, but that much of this wealth was not being used effectively for the benefit of the community.

In response to the findings of the Sachar Committee, the Indian government undertook several initiatives to improve the management of Waqf properties. These included the establishment of the National Waqf Development Corporation (NAWADCO) in 2013, which was tasked with developing Waqf

CHAPTER XVIII

How To Cope With Reforms?

Islam's law of inheritance is once again under discussion. Debates for and against Sharia law in general and inheritance law in particular are taking place on social media. It is the descendants of those who fought against the Islamic Sharia in the eighties, and now the first shot has been fired against the succession law in Islam. The law of inheritance in Islam is against the modern concept of equality. Succession law in Islam has been criticized in the past for highlighting the 'inequality' of the male-female share. The argument against gender equality is the universal declaration of the Holy Qur'an that 'the share of a man is equal to the share of two women' (Qur'an 4:11). Therefore, some have come forward with the argument that it should be revised in time. While one group argues for Sharia reform, there is another argument that Sharia is not subject to any change as it is divinely inspired. In the channel discussions that followed the controversy, those demanding reform of Sharia laws also claimed that many such reforms had taken place in the Muslim world. However, this discussion taken up by the media in India has opened up opportunities for people to learn more about Islamic Sharia in general and succession law in particular.

In this regard, the first question that needs to be answered is whether Sharia laws change over time. If so, will the law of inheritance be among the laws that undergo reform? Has Sharia law been modified in modern times? This article is an inquiry into what they are, if any.

Basics That Don't Change And Details That Change

When asked whether Sharia laws change over time, the simple answer is that there are laws that change and permanent laws that never change. Compared to religious or man-made legal systems, the main characteristic of Islamic Sharia can be seen in its immutable fundamentals and changeable details. In Islamic Sharia, there are aspects (Variables) that are subject to change according to space and time changes, and fundamentals (Fundamentals) that are never subject to change. Unchanging Fundamentals and Changing Variables, Eternal Fundamentals and Flexible Details, Scholars interpret that feature in many ways. The foundations of Islamic Sharia are divine and therefore eternal and relevant in all regions. But, in its branchial aspects, these principles and laws relate to human life and can take practical and contemporary forms according to the needs of man's space-time conditions. They are subject to change. Beyond divine revelation, it is the place of ijtihad, which uses human intellect to arrive at judgments, positions and approaches.

There are some fixed factors and some changing factors in humans. Islam also has two sides like this. and aspects that are constant and subject to change and modification. The six articles of faith and the five articles of ritual are the foundations of Islam that never change. Human-moral-ethical values also remain unchanged. Truth, Dharma, Justice and Mercy are the highest values of all times and all lands. Generally, devotional activities are permanent and human dealings (*Mu'amalat*) are reformative in nature. However, the Muslim world sees the Islamic penal laws (*Hudud*) and inheritance laws, which are decreed in the Qur'an, as fixed commands for all time without change. They are not judgments that change with the changes of space and time.

The purpose of Shariah laws is the welfare and prosperity of mankind. Its laws are intended to provide either material or spiritual good to man. In that sense, the rulings of Shariah, including the law of inheritance, are for human welfare. All the goodness intended by Allah should be available through it. However, social, economic and political conditions change from time to time. In such circumstances, the carnal legal system will stand in the way of human progress. It will need to be updated from time to time. However, Islamic Sharia has the capacity to accommodate and cope with these changes without compromising the fundamentals. The Usooli scholars, taking into account this peculiarity of the Sharia, enunciated the principle that the fatwa will change according to the change of time and space conditions. Otherwise, the change of time and space conditions will lead to the change of Sharia rulings. However, these changes will not be manifested on the grounds that the Holy Qur'an has categorically prescribed. On the contrary, these changes will be in matters of ijtihad that are not directly mentioned in the Qur'an and Sunnah.

Reforms In Personal And Family Laws

Sharia reform does not mean the complete abolition of Sharia law. As mentioned above, the subject of ijtihad changes according to the changes in space and time. In that sense, individual-family-marital-succession laws have been reformed in countries like Turkey, Egypt, Tunisia, undivided India and Indonesia. The Ottoman Law of Family Rights (OLFR), codified in 1917, is known as the first reform initiative in personal law in the Muslim world. It has been accused of being a state-sponsored construction by European influence. However, the truth is that many of the revised laws brought about by the new codification did not negate the basic principles of Islamic Sharia. They were transformative laws. However, many new ideas and lifestyles brought by modernity led to the reformation of Sharia laws.

The Tunisian Law of Personal Status enacted in Tunisia in 1956 criminalized polygamy. The members of the Law Committee interpreted the sharia's conditional permission to marry up to four times as making it absolutely impossible for a man to do justice in this regard. But the enactment of the Qur'an, without regard to its express permission, was construed to mean that the condition mentioned therein could not be complied with, and led to widespread objections. Since the 1920s, many laws have been enacted in Egypt to reduce polygamy. Since the 1960s, second marriages have only been possible in Egypt with the permission of the court. According to the 1917 OLFR, if a husband marries a second time without the consent of his first wife, the marriage was considered null and void.

Definitions of '*Nushuz*' (disobedience to husband) in the light of European laws are also considered as a reform in family law. While in pre-modern Fiqh '*Nushuz*' was generally limited to bedroom disobedience, a woman's failure in other responsibilities was also considered 'Nushus' in the revised law. Muslim personal law in Algeria states that if a woman does not respect her husband as the head of the family, that too falls within the scope of disobedience. Going a step further in Morocco, a husband's failure to honour his parents would also fall under the purview of '*Nushuz*'.

Premodern Fiqh was that if the husband failed to look after the family, the woman could divorce her husband after one year. However, Article 116 of the OLFR made an amendment to it. Accordingly, if a woman wants to divorce her husband, one year of non-payment of expenses is not enough; four years is required. The law has also been amended several times to raise the marriageable age of girls and boys. In short, most of the reforms in Muslim personal law in the OLFR were curtailing women's rights. Its peculiarity was that the laws were modified so that in matters which could affect only one person or his family, they came under the control and monitoring of the state.

In Fiqh prior to European contact, the male was not considered the centre of authority in the family. Muslim women were more independent and had rights in personal and economic matters. The husband had no legal right over his wife's wealth. A woman had no additional obligation to respect her husband's parents beyond the way her husband respected his parents. Wael Hallaq observes that the general character of the reform in Muslim law following European colonization was that it was male-centred and reluctant to grant women property rights after marriage. These laws were male-centred due to the influence of the French Civil Code, which was the source of recent legal reform in Muslim countries.

Reforms In Inheritance Laws

in the field of inheritance, laws were mostly done by adopting the Takhayyur and Talfiq (selection and amalgamation) methods.

Takhayyur means accepting a new opinion by combining the weakest opinion of one's own madhhab with the opinions of other madhhabs.

The general rule among the Sunnis is that a daughter whose father is deceased, if she has a paternal brother, should be divided equally between the daughter and the paternal brother. But among the Isna Asharis, the daughter inherits the property. The Sunnis also follow this practice today by adopting this practice of the Isna Ashari Shiites through Takhayyur. The majority of Iraq's Sunnis and Kurds follow this rule.

Thinkers influenced by modernism like Muhammad Shahrur gave another interpretation to the verse of the Holy Qur'an (4:11). In Shahrur's view, through this verse Allah has declared the highest and the lowest amount of share between men and women. Regardless of who is the head of the family, the share of the woman should not be reduced at all from what the Qur'an has said here. The male portion should not exceed even a little from the amount mentioned in the Qur'an. According to it, under no circumstances shall the share of women be less than 33.33 per cent or the share of men more than 66.6 per cent. Therefore, give 40% share to the woman and 60% to the man in the inheritance. When that happens, the upper limit set by Allah for the male share and the lower limit set for the female share will not be violated. But keeping Shahrur's opinion in mind, Sharia law is not known to have been revised anywhere in the world. It was considered as an isolated interpretation of the said verse.

The Egyptian Law of Testamentary Disposition (ELTD), which came into force in Egypt in 1946, was also a law reform in the division of inheritance. All these reforms were in ijma' of the leading scholars of all the four Madhhabs who lived at that time. According to this, the rules came through ELTD that no property can be transferred to heirs through will, only one-third of the property can be considered for will, and those who receive property through inheritance should not be considered for will.

The New Law In Tunisia

Modern calls for equal rights for men and women to inherit property began in Tunisia. The Tunisian parliament considered introducing such a law in 2018. In August 2017, the then President of Tunisia, Baji Quaid Sabzi, formed a committee called the Committee on Individual Rights and Equality to study the individual rights of the people of the country. On June 1, 2018, this committee submitted a 235-page report calling for reforms in the rights of citizens and amending the existing 1956 Personal Acts in the country based on the recommendations of the committee. One of the recommendations of this committee was that men and women should have equal rights in inheritance. After the Jasmine Revolution, Under the 2014 constitution, such a law would have to be debated and voted on in parliament. However, the law was not passed in Parliament that year due to the opposition of the opposition and the public. A report found that 52% of women and 75% of men opposed the reform of the Islamic inheritance law. Prominent scholars of the country and organizations like Annahda have opposed the reform.

Attitude Towards Reforms

Sharia law reforms in the Muslim world have some that are acceptable and some that are not. The mechanism for shaping the believer's approach to new situations and problems as they arise in society is part of the Deen itself. That is Ijtihad. The religious judgments, approaches and positions reached by the scholars of different periods through ijtihad point to the development orientation of the Sharia to accommodate the demands of the time and space conditions. This is the aspect of change of Sharia mentioned above. The Muslim world has always accepted such ijtihads of scholars. Shaykh Abu Zahra observes that the general reform of family and personal laws in the early twentieth century in the Muslim world was to bring in laws that were suitable for the people and were closer to the needs of the times. For that, the rules were taken from the four prominent madhhabs. When such a reform was introduced in Egypt in 1915, the law reform committee included scholars representing all four madhhabs. Unlike premodern Fiqh, such reforms were made with the knowledge and consent of the leading scholars of all madhhabs, and the universal sharia laws adopted by the Muslim world.

There have also been reforms in Muslim countries that were not accepted by the Muslim world. It is not correct to judge all laws enacted by Muslim rulers as legitimate reforms of the Sharia. In the name of reform, attempts have also been made in Muslim countries to overturn the stable foundations and immutable laws of Sharia. Following colonization, the Muslim world witnessed many reforms influenced by Western values. Such 'reforms' by rulers who dared blindly imitate the West were being imposed amid great opposition from the Muslim world. There were rulers who banned Muslim symbols like the bank, hijab and beard. There have also been rulers who openly discouraged fasting during Ramadan. All those measures were reforms for them. But none of them can be considered Islamic legal reforms adopted by the Muslim world. Scholars in the Islamic world and the Muslim masses have a history of opposing such reforms by Muslim rulers who were in servitude to the European occupying powers. This new law passed by the Tunisian parliament, which seeks to once again embrace ultra-secularism, is one such case.

GENDER DEBATES

CHAPTER XIX

Muslim Women And Personal Law In India: Debates And Struggles

There are three things that should be noted in the debates related to Muslim personal laws. First, the diversity of Muslim women's living conditions. Two, the characteristics of Islam. Third, the constitution and laws of the countries where Muslims live. By integrating and considering these three things, we need to devise political programs that provide justice and equal opportunities for Muslim women. A detailed debate should be opened after appropriating all these realities. It is mentioned in the book 'Gender and Equality in Muslim Family Law: Justice and Ethics in the Islamic Legal tradition', edited by Mir Hussaini, that the historical diversity of Islamic law, which is a part of Islamic Sharia itself, should be counted in present debates.

Parliament session has sparked new controversies on issues such as the Uniform Civil Code, the gender status of Muslim women and the right to self-determination of the Muslim minority. Independent Muslim women's organization called Bharatiya Muslim Mahila Andolan has conducted a nationwide campaign against oppression of Indian Muslim women. They advocated reforming Muslim personal law by banning anti-women Muslim personal laws. In view of this case and the subsequent debate, two main types of reactions have emerged.

One: To protect Muslim women from anti-feminist personal laws, a single civil code should be implemented banning personal laws. This view is advanced by right-wing nationalists and some religious/secular feminists.

Two: Against this, various Muslim organizations, thinkers and feminists who are part of mass politics came forward and argued for the protection of Muslim personal law.

In this context, Flavia Agnes and Nivedita Menon, leading voices in the field of women's politics in India, observe that not a single feminist civil code, but a Hinduized code, is trying to be imposed on India's minority marginalized community, and should be countered. It is very clear that even feminists in India are moving away from pure individualism that obscures Hindu upper class women's privileges and are now talking about structures including community.

In this situation, the equation of Muslim personal law and women's rights needs to be analysed a little more closely. Ever since the much-discussed Shah Bano case of 1985, the demand for a single civil code to protect Muslim women from the barbarities of anti-modern religious law has been growing. Divorced after forty-three years of marriage in 1978, sixty-two-year-old Shah Bano filed a petition in the Madhya Pradesh Indore Magistrate's Court seeking maintenance from her husband. Although the judgment came in their favour, they appealed to the High Court to get a little more alimony. The High Court increased the alimony to Rs.179.20. But her husband, Muhammad Ahmad Khan, filed a petition in the Supreme Court on the basis that under Muslim personal law, no alimony is payable after the first three months of divorce (technically known as iddah).

But the Supreme Court also ruled in Shah Bano's favour, according to Section 125 of the Criminal Procedure Act, 1973. All India Muslim organizations came forward declaring that this verdict is a challenge to the very existence of Muslim personal law. In February 1986 as a result of the meeting Muslim leaders had with then Prime Minister Rajiv Gandhi (Muslim women (Protection of Rights on Divorce) Act) came into force. Accordingly, the Muslim woman was exempted from the benefit of Criminal Procedure Code 125 and the period for payment of alimony was reduced to three months (idda period). Various women's organizations and writers have come forward pointing out that this violates the rights given to women by the constitution.

However, the Muslim Women (Protection of Rights to Divorce) Act has created confusion in adjudicating the matter by requiring settlements to be paid within three months in many of the later cases. That is, it was not possible to arrive at a unilateral decision as to whether the alimony should be paid for three months only or for the future.

Danial Latifi Case

Shah Bano's lawyer Danial Latifi filed a public interest petition in the Supreme Court questioning the validity of the Muslim Women (Protection of Divorce) Act. Although the judgment of the case came in 2001, the Danial Latifi case played a major role in bringing a new dimension to the Muslim Women (Protection of Divorce) Act. The Supreme Court ruled that alimony should be paid after taking into account the settlement amount after the three-month period.

The Dania Latifi case is notable for several reasons.

One: Muslim organizations including the Muslim Personal Law Board have not publicly protestested against this judgement . But Flavia Agnes criticizes the mainstream media for not giving enough attention to the verdict. Because with this ruling, there was no opportunity for a political controversy, because the ruling was malleable for all.

Two: If you study the judgment of Danial Latifi case, Nivedita Menon observes how progressive it is from the condition of Hindu women who have to undergo chastity test every month to get alimony under the existing Hindu code bill.

A comparison of Sha Banu, Danial Latifi and Shayara Banu cases will make it clear that the judgments are being discussed in our public sphere in many ways. Court judgments themselves are used in many ways as part of political debate here. The current public debate on this issue, however, stems from ignorance of the history of legal debates about Muslim women. The stereotype of the victimized Muslim woman has always been a part of our public imagination. Court rulings contradicting it make news, but different court rulings in this regard go unnoticed. A comparative study of the Sha Banu, Danial Latifi and Shayara Banu cases shows that the

Muslim community or community organizations have not adopted uniform approaches to all court judgments.

As Flavia Agnes points out, there have already been several court rulings invalidating triple talaq. Danial Latifi case is not an exception. Notable among them are the judgment of Guwahati High Court in 1981 before the Shah Banocase and the judgment of the Shamim Ara case in 2002. These provide an explanation of the divorce procedure based on Islamic principles. A mediation session involving both parties must be convened before a divorce can be filed. Then the divorce should be announced in front of witnesses. Then after the three-month Idda period, if there is no possibility of reunification, the divorce becomes complete. It should be noted that dowry violence and other domestic violence come under the scope of Domestic Violence Act, 2005 and should not be confused with personal law. In this way, Flavia Agnes questions the logic of politicizing personal problem in the family as the problem of Muslim women and the community as a whole. Moreover, the selective use of law and court judgment itself reveals its bias.

What Flavia Agnes says links Muslim personal law debates to a more detailed political context. It helps us to see the debate about Muslim personal law as a problem of the development of modernity through the law of the nation, and also as a problem of modern structures of power such as the nation, nationhood, the state, colonial modernity, and the politics of law. Therefore, it does not seem possible to reduce the civil code debate to the absolute sense to the problem of pre-modern religion and modern gender politics.

Politics Of Uniform Civil Code

The uniform Civil Code debate is aligned with the political interests of Hindu Rashtra construction through the formulation of upper-caste Hindu nationalism. Social acceptance for this goal has been achieved by creating a common sense of 'Indianizing' the Muslim and Christian communities. It helps to assess the Single Civil Code as part of modern power struggles in Indian politics, apart from being simply a Muslim women's rights issue. Part of these modern power struggles is the Muslim Personal Law Board, which is now accused of standing in direct opposition to the interests of Muslim women in the public imagination.

For example, let us examine how the All India Muslim Personal Law Board was constituted. In 1972, HR Gokhale, the Law Minister in Indira Gandhi's cabinet, presented the demand for a general adoption law in Parliament. He argued that it should be applied equally to all communities. On the adopted child till he reaches the age of majority Muslim personal law dictates that adoptees have the right to be legal guardians. Various Muslim organizations and religious leaders have viewed the move by law minister as an action that disregards instructions in the Muslim Personal Law. As a result of Muslim leaders coming together to discuss this, the All India Muslim Personal Law Board came into existence in 1973, raising the demand that Muslim personal law should be protected. The political and constitutional rights of the Muslim minority in India were part of the board's founding objectives. This politics of communal self-determination is also the background of the violent anti-Muslim riots in India in the late sixties.

Later, in the Shah Banocase, Justice YV Chandrachud's remarks criticizing the Muslim Personal Law caused another controversy. Before that, in 1984, the Madras High Court and Justice Krishna Iyer, from the perspective of social justice, had ruled in favour of Muslim women for monthly alimony. None of these have caused controversy. At that time, no Muslim organization had ever come with a protest like today. But why the Shah Banocase became controversial politically? What is its background?

Two main things determine the uniform civil code debate today. Both are issues of national self-determination that haunted the very formation of the Indian nation-state and its colonial history. By analysing them, a different picture will be available for the debate on the single civil code.

Doctrinal Struggles, Babri Masjid And Shah Bano Case

A.G. Noorani says in his study 'The Muslims of India: A Documentary Record' that the Shah Bano case and the Muslim Women's Act implemented after that should be analysed in conjunction with the opening of the doors of the Babri Masjid in Ayodhya to Hindus. On March 8, 1986, on Shivaratri, Rajiv Gandhi decided to open the gates of the Babri Masjid saying that it was the birthplace of Ram. Just before this, in the month of February, Rajiv Gandhi passed the Muslim Women's Bill in the Parliament. Left and right elite Hindu consciousness in India believed that Rajiv Gandhi was appeasing the Muslim community. The Ram Janmabhoomi Mukti Samiti led by the Vishwa Hindu Parishad is in this situation resolved the decision to open the gates of Masjid by force protesting Muslim appeasement politics of Congress.

In this context, Muslim leaders saw the decision to open the doors of the Babri Masjid to the Vishwa Hindu Parishad as part of Rajiv Gandhi's political move rather than religious commitment. The VHP alleged that the decision to pass the Muslim Women's Bill was like Rajiv Gandhi repeating the mistakes made by Gandhi and Nehru in the case of Muhammad Ali Jinnah. So, under the pressure of VHP, Rajiv Gandhi opened the Babri Masjid to them the very next month.

There is another background to this. In the 1980s, when the Dalit masses began to self-organize, the power of Hindu Brahminical politics declined with the conversion of Dalits to Islam in Tamil Nadu's Meenakshipuram. Noorani also observes that with this the Sangh Parivar forces started devising new strategies for Hindu unification. Babari mobilization was a move against Dalit Bahujan politics. It is a part of this that the Shah Bano case, unlike many other similar cases, has become a big political controversy and joins political issues including the Babri Masjid. To link it only to gender politics is a historical misreading.

Therefore, those working in the field of Muslim women's politics in India should adopt an intersectional approach. The Shah Bano case opens up the possibility of Islamic feminist politics. That is, the history of the Shah Bano case urges us to contextually and specifically address the multiple structures of alienation and oppression of Muslim women without simply reducing the critique to the fact that Muslim women are oppressed by men in the Muslim community in all times and places. This is a recognition historically achieved by at least some sections of feminist politics in India. But in saying this we must develop some clear understanding of the workings of Muslim personal law. Let's give some pointers for that.

The Origin And Development Of Personal Law In The Modern Nation

The current uniform civil code promotes the politics of Hindu caste supremacy. India's neo-democratic polity has reached some degree of consensus on this issue. Along with that, the possibility of decolonizing existing Muslim personal law as a by-product of colonial legislation needs to be examined.

The codification of personal laws was implemented by the British nation-state during the colonial era, rejecting pluralism within various communities. Subsequently, the post-colonial Indian constitution recognized the personal laws of five communities such as Hindu, Muslim, Christian, Parsi, and Jew and the tribal laws of Hindus. Marriage, divorce, inheritance, alimony, guardianship, adoption, death certificate etc. are specifically covered by personal laws. Rajeshwari Sundar Rajan in her article 'Women between Community and State: Some Implications of the Uniform Civil Code Debates in India' has assessed that all community laws in general retain a male-centric and anti-feminist character.

At the same time, the tendency to read Muslim personal law as the embodiment of Shria has to be challenged. That is, we need to understand the changes coming to Sharia in the modern administrative system of nation-state. For example, Hallaq observes that the law was conceived in pre-modern Islamic societies as a means to achieve the ethical and moral goals intended by the Shariah and the administrative systems that were part of that society. But, later it was apportioned by states to get the leeway of legitimization among the civil society.

But as the colonial nations gained dominance over the Muslim social/administrative system, the legal aspect of Sharia gained importance and its moral and ethical purpose was forgotten. Sharia has been reduced to the politics of legislation that is the cornerstone of modern nation-states. We should note that the studies of the likes of Hallaq point out that Sharia is an ethical and moral framework that modern regimes failed to assimilate . These differences are historical insights that must be considered in discussions of what Sharia has to do with the Muslim individuals today.

Unfortunately, in the tumult of modern political controversy, the intellectual probity and thoughtfulness necessary to engage in such discussions are not available today. The media that controls all this does not even inquire how the majority of Muslim women live in Islam. Thus, the space to see the Muslim women's problem from within Islam shrinks and the Muslim women's life is reduced to the state and legislation.

The Way Forward

The above discussion clarifies two things. One of them is that today's Muslim personal law is a creation of colonial modernity. At the same time, the second fact is that the uniform civil code debate going on now is a re-creation of Upper caste morals. Therefore, in today's situation, while rejecting the Uniform Civil Code completely, we need to reject the colonial construction of Muslim personal law. In his study 'Speaking in God's Name : Islamic Law, Authority and Women', Khalid Abou El Fadl says that the current nature of Muslim personal law does not even consider the rights given to women by Islamic Sharia. But Muslim/non-Muslim women's institutions also suffer from limitations in addressing this conflict.

An important voice in Islamic feminist politics, Ziba Mir-Hosseini, an Iranian Islamic feminist who has done extensive research on issues of women's authority within Islamic law, has studied Muslim personal law in various parts of the world and proposed alternatives. Their propositions generally provide significant insights for those working in the field of Muslim women's politics in India.

Ziba Mir-Hosseini argues that the basis of injustice in extant interpretations of Islamic law is not divine, but a construct of male jurists. This, they say, creates two possibilities: epistemological and political. The first point of view of Ziba Mir-Hosseini is that many of the laws that are now considered as part of Sharia are only the views and social habits of some Muslim communities and Muslim men and therefore, they can be subject to change. Second, it frees Muslims from adopting a defensive stance and helps them to transcend old Islamic legal frameworks and discover new questions and answers.

There are three things that should be noted in the debates related to Muslim personal laws. First, the diversity of Muslim women's living conditions. Two, the characteristics of Islam. Third, the constitution and laws of the countries where Muslims live. By integrating and considering these three things, we need to devise political programs that provide justice and equal opportunities for Muslim women. A detailed debate should be opened after appropriating all these realities. It is mentioned in the book 'Gender and Equality in Muslim Family Law: Justice and Ethics in the Islamic Legal tradition', edited by Mir Hussaini, that the historical diversity of Islamic law, which is a part of Islamic Sharia itself, should be counted in present debates.

CHAPTER XX

Muslim Women In Public Space

There are several limitations to distinguishing Muslim women's lives as authorship/non-authority: first, this method is insufficient to understand the lives of Muslim women who see Islam as important. Second, this approach refuses to see the power structures such as caste/religion/state/economy/region that affect the Muslim woman's life. Therefore, it is not possible to embrace the life of Muslim women who stand with the community and clash with other power structures through this approach. Third, criticisms raised by Muslim women from within the community are very quickly hijacked and cause public discourse to be organized against the community. Fourth, it denies the possibility of a different existence for the communal life of the Muslim woman.

The politics of what is written from the women's point of view in Kerala's mainstream newspapers, weeklies and magazines and the responses about Muslim women in social media and channel discussions are under consideration here. This article attempts to discuss the possibilities and dilemmas of feminist narratives centred on Muslim women as part of religious minority/Islamic/Muslim politics.

The Problem Of Methodology: Excess And Absence

The field of women's theories and politics in Kerala is too complex to be tied into a single thread. Liberal, Marxist, Radical, Christian, Muslim, Adivasi, Dalit, upper caste Hindu and different feminist trends are strong in Kerala. At the same time, public discourse in Kerala is seen to follow liberal/Hindu upper caste politics knowingly or unknowingly.

Discussions are going on at various levels based on the Muslim woman's body, sexuality and social status such as education, occupation, dress, marriage, age of marriage. But in such discussions, the main factor that determines the authorship of a

Muslim woman will be the religion, the community or the Muslim man. Therefore, the Muslim woman is represented in public discussions in two ways: First, as a victim who does not quarrel with her own community and is therefore oppressed by the Muslim man. Two, the warrior who fights alone with his own community and the Muslim man.

There are several limitations to distinguishing Muslim women's lives as authorship/non-authority: first, this method is insufficient to understand the lives of Muslim women who see Islam as important. Second, this approach refuses to see the power structures such as caste/religion/state/economy/region that affect the Muslim woman's life. Therefore, it is not possible to embrace the life of Muslim women who stand with the community and clash with other power structures through this approach. Third, criticisms raised by Muslim women from within the community are very quickly hijacked and cause public discourse to be organized against the community. Fourth, it denies the possibility of a different existence for the communal life of the Muslim woman.

Even knowing that the above is true, the way forward is not that easy. My personal assessment in the Muslim Women Studies Center is that there is a lot of difficulty in bringing what we know and experience while studying Muslim women into the realm of language and discourse. The way out of this is an abundance of writings that can take the Muslim women's experience seriously and bring out the dilemmas of our thinking. At the same time, it must develop into a new critical consciousness that does not fall into the trap of absolute empiricism. It is a relief that today there is a small number of Muslim women writers and a Muslim women research community taking up this challenge.

Frameworks Of Rights Politics

As mentioned earlier, the complexities of Muslim women's rights politics are generally discussed in conjunction with the politics of masculinity in the Muslim community. This oneIt is a method seen worldwide. Laila Abu-Lughd in her Do Muslim Women Need Saving? (Harvard University Press 2014) writes about a conversation with Zainab, a Muslim woman from a village in Egypt. Zainab, who makes a living by farming and trading to support her family, is aware of the hardships she faces as a Muslim woman. But she cites the government's non-subsidy and corrupt officials in her country more than Islam as the cause of her hardship. In other words, the criticism of Muslim men should be prepared to be freed from its satanic approaches.

This problem exists in many ways in Kerala too. Campaigns and books have been launched for Muslim women's right to education in Kerala and Vishishya Malabar based on Malala, who was shot by the Taliban in Pakistan. Many seminars were also held on women's right to education. Women politicians including PK Mrs. have intervened and spoken on this issue.

However, no one was ready to support the struggles or to suggest ways to solve the problems related to the backwardness of Malabar's right to education. No one discussed the educational rights that the democratic regime here did not grant to Muslim women. Even the left-wing women's organizations spoke for Malala by skillfully covering up the fact that the backwardness of Malabar would make the Muslim women here backward. They talked about the violation of Muslim women's rights on the Pak-Afghan border by not providing facilities to an ordinary Muslim girl in Malappuram to study.

Is the discrimination and denial of rights of Muslim women related to education and employment only religious? How many women engineering colleges are there in the Malappuram district where majority of Muslim women live? Existing Govt. What is the number of women's colleges? Has the government here done as much as Muslim community organizations have done for the advancement of Muslim women's education? Isn't it the Muslim community itself that runs good quality English medium schools in Malappuram where many Muslim girls study? These questions, which complicate the politics of Muslim women's rights, are rarely seen in our public discourse. Because these questions break the stereotype of the 'Muslim woman whose rights are suppressed only by religion'.

Muslim Women And Elections

A major debate in feminist studies is the issue of what women's choice is. Certainly, there is no free choice. Election is possible only from within any structure. But a political assessment of the election is possible. Therefore, the important question is who decides what is the right choice in public discourse.

At the same time, we should note that the liberal politics of election is also emerging as part of this discussion. A discussion of how feminist studies and the public discourses that develop around it view the liberal politics of choice is crucial. Nadia Fadil and Talal Asad have examined this issue in detail. My focus is on the particularities of debates about elections as seen in public discourse in Kerala. How to understand the choices made by women who see religion as important? Why do a large number of Muslim women still choose Islam? Why is this election not an election? These are the questions our public discourses must still face.

Women who choose their religion do not have much space in public discourses related to women in Kerala. Apart from the general media, this discrimination can be easily understood if one examines the magazines and discussion forums run by feminists in Kerala. How can women who choose a particular religion and the lifestyles associated with it come out of women's choice? For example, to what extent is it possible for our public discourse to recognize a Muslim woman who wears a hijab, a Muslim woman who is part of Muslim organizations / has an Islamic lifestyle, as a woman with a voice and space?

Feminists of all kinds are coming in a lot in discussions led by Muslim women. They get a lot of opportunity to interact with Muslim women. Women's organizations including Jamaat-e-Islami invite all kinds of feminists to debate. But do feminists treat women whose religion is important that way? What is the participation of Muslim women who see religion as important in their arenas and follow its beliefs and practices? Are feminist media as inclusive of women for whom Islam is important as other women?

But the same question can be asked about religion. Whose interest comes out as a choice of religion? Who determines religion and its choices? A more critical approach to these issues needs to be developed. No level of ultimatum should be adopted.

When Is There A Muslim Women Problem?

When is the Muslim women's issue framed as a Muslim women's issue? Another issue criticized is Arabic wedding and Mysore wedding. They consider these to be the responsibility of the Muslim religious establishment. Observations that draw conclusions so easily have several limitations.

The media itself says that the Mysore wedding is also related to 'dowry'. This problem mostly affects poor Muslim women. Dowry is often cited as the main reason by the media itself (and how dowry works in different women's situations needs to be looked at closely).

But the Islamic organizations take a strong stand against dowry by expelling members who get married after buying 'dowry'. Are organizations like DYFI and Youth Congress ready to take such a stand against dowry? In this sense, why place the responsibility of the problems in Muslim societies 'solely' on the shoulders of Islamic organizations? Is the misogyny of a Muslim working in DYFI a problem for Islam?

Another fact is that people never . No one mentions the increased participation of Muslim women students in professional colleges in Kerala as a 'good thing' for Muslim organizations. But social injustices like the Mysore marriage are too easily conflated with the 'religious' uniqueness of the Muslim and seen as 'evil'. Aren't economic structures, social/political movements, religious and secular forms of masculinity at play in this injustice? Feminist readings often succumb to a secular logic in which the Muslim's 'guilt' is only religion.

Most influential progressives in our public life tend to make the Muslim women's issue special. This tendency was often sharpened during the Fascist period. Many people think that the secular criticism against fascism in India will be complete only if the violence perpetrated by Muslims all over the world is exposed. Many people talk about Muslim politics and Muslims as victims of fascism by making excuses.

Muslim women are the main instrument of anti-fascist discourse built on weak foundations. Activists and writers with positions and powers therefore, after taking two or three pro-Muslim positions, they will come out with a fourth anti-Muslim position due to their guilt. They will do it by using the Muslim woman as a tool. There are very few progressives in Kerala who do not fall into the victimized Muslim woman/violent Muslim man equation.

Whose Control And Whose Freedom?

The classification of secular restrictions on Muslim women as good and religious restrictions as bad is often seen in public discourse. In educational settings today there are many restrictions on the hijab, purdah, and niqab of Muslim women. It never analyzes public discourse as a controlling authority. Similarly, women who choose to wear the purdah and hijab are not seen . Restrictions on a Muslim woman's dress in public are generally not considered restrictions.

Remember CBSE asked to remove Hijab in All India Medical Entrance Exam. It called for a secular education system to control Muslim women. But it did not cause much concern or discussion in public discourse. Because it is the government that says what a Muslim woman should wear. The discussion proceeded as if the secular Muslim men who supported the ban, the state and the mainstream Indian media had no problem with male authority.

In the Indian context, not only religions but also the state, discourses such as feminism are in the realm of power. Women's power itself has in many cases worked hand-in-hand with superior power. In that sense, public discourse reduces regulatory authority to a problem of Islam alone.

Representations Of The Muslim Woman: Distance And Intimacy

Why are oppressed Muslim women's experiences living at a distance so abundant in Kerala's literary market? Ayan Hirsi Ali and others are part of our common culture. Moreover, stories from afar are reported only when the violence of the Muslim community is inflicted on a Muslim woman. The wretched lives of the hundreds of thousands of Muslim women killed by the occupation forces in Iraq and Afghanistan are not part of this market industry. Their voices are not heard in public discourses. Moreover, the media searched for local events in Kerala that were similar to the experiences in the distanceYou can see the news. Thus again following the same steps of global politics, the media here is building orientalist models with Muslim women in mind.

The experiences of Zakaria's mother Biumma, who has been in Agrahara jail for the past eight years, Sufiya Madani, who was branded a terrorist and hunted down because she was the wife of Abdulnasir Madani, Sirajunnisa, who was killed by the police during Advani's Ratha Yatra, the women of the families of those who were branded as terrorists and imprisoned, and the women who were victims of the terror regime in Bimapally, do not become big stories in public discourse. Because they are telling us a different story. They speak very organically from us. We don't see those stories in the commotion that makes public literature/media discourse. It requires different political and social frameworks.

The New Politics Of The Muslim Woman

If we write openly about Muslim women and their lives, there is a threat that it will be used by the liberal politics or advocates of supremacy here. Therefore, many people are silent on the issue of Muslim women. Many Muslim women are at a loss as to how to develop a language of community critique away from hegemonic politics. But the fact is that by remaining silent, Muslim women are silencing themselves. Often what Muslim women write or say is not read. In the presence of many stereotypes about the Muslim community, politics is analyzed by selecting prejudiced notions.

Some of the successful practical political models offer the experiences of Muslim women. By being able to bring the Muslim women's issue as part of the unity of different types of subordinate communities and women's politics within it, the possibility of communitarian women's politics is developing. Instead of silencing ourselves by thinking about the tactics of the dominant politics, we need to develop brotherhoods with those who know about Muslim women's issues. Thus it is to be hoped that by making new combinations the judgments of the common law may be overruled.

Rarely are there spaces to think and think differently about Muslim women. Therefore, it is necessary to build a new political imagination while agreeing with women and communities who are experiencing problems like Muslim women. Such efforts simultaneously serve to bring to light the dominant tendencies of women's politics and the subordinate nature of the Muslim community.

CHAPTER XXI

The Hijab: Beyond Oppression And Liberation

Hijab helps Muslim women who choose hijab in situations where Muslims are in the minority, to stop their social, religious and gender differences. But it is my personal experience that if a woman wears a "hijab" in a "secular" place like Indian universities, she is subjected to secular moral policing as either a "Kashmiri/ traitor" or "oppressed by religious tradition". In his book "The Islamic Veil: Beginners Guide" the author Elizabeth Bucar puts forward some subtle observations.

Muslim women's dress is widely discussed in the world today. The secularists leading this discussion are evaluating the role of the Muslim woman as a product of oppression, anarchism and irrationality. At the same time, this is understood as a religious problem within the Muslim community. Moreover, in modern times, as a response to secularism, a way of seeing Muslim women's clothing as a liberating agenda has also developed from the religious side. Unlike these two, many academic studies are now coming out related to the perception of Muslim women's clothing in different geographical-social-political-cultural environments. In such a religious and secular environment, "The Islamic Veil: Beginners Guide", published by Oneworld Publications in 2012, is a book that examines the possibilities and impossibilities of the approaches in the light of new academic research. The author is Elizabeth Bucar, an assistant professor in religious studies at North Eastern University in the United States. Her earlier Iran-focused studies of Muslim women and sexuality have been well noted. Her works on ethics, precepts, law, colonialism, education, work, and personality have provided a new structure to academic studies.

The book consists of eight chapters containing debates related to the hijab and fashion. Throughout the book, the English word "Islamic Veil" is used for Islamic dress. She discusses the hijab, veil, khimar, jilbab, and niqab, which represent the clothing of Muslim women living in different situations, and the turban and face covering used by Muslim men of the Tuareg tribe in Morocco. In this book, Elizabeth Bucar adopted the word, Islamic Veil, taking into account the Muslim dress as a whole, including women and men. For ease of understanding, the word "Hijab" is used in this article to refer to the head covering of Muslim women in India.

Three main reasons led Bucar to write this book. One) The role of the Muslim woman is in the first place in the debates related to women's freedom in the world today. That is why this issue needs to be subjected to serious debate. 2) An attempt to highlight the different approaches Muslim women take towards clothing. Bucar observes that Muslim women in the same situation still need to learn how to approach Islamic dress in different ways. In 2004, she spoke to women leaders of organizations fighting for women's political rights in Iran. Not one of them spoke of the Islamic State's compulsory dress code for Muslim women in Iran as a rights issue. Moreover, they adopted a very "conventional" dress code. But unlike them, Bucar observes that young women in the city who are interested in modern fashion are speaking out against the government's mandated dress code. 3) In the mainstream debates, there are very one-sided discussions regarding the perception of Muslim women's clothing. They reduce Muslim women's dress to an agenda of religious fundamentalism. This is a debate that does not consider what the Muslim woman says about herself and her dress. In these debates, secular male-female feminists and Muslim men often argue about what constitutes a "Muslim woman." Through this, a religious and social entity called "Muslim woman" is forgotten and rendered invisible. Although many field studies have been conducted to investigate what Muslim woman says about themselves, it does not receive enough attention. Instead, the Muslim woman is relegated to being a product of wishful thinking shared by secular feminism and Muslim men.

Hijab-related debates/controversies arise as a historical situation with the colonial conquests that took place in the Islamic world. Colonialism as a political practice and Orientalism as part of began to talk about Muslim dress. Bucar argues that the debates about clothing and Muslim women's clothing that we see today were formed when liberal feminism as part of elite women's rights politics in Euro-America surrendered to these agendas.

Colonialism And Sartorial Rights Of Muslim Women

The role played by Islam in the struggles and defences against the occupation in Muslim-majority countries was a major setback for the colonial powers. The colonial powers justified their invasion by saying that we do not want the land of the Muslims but that they should somehow be reformed and become good people. Saving the Muslim woman from the violent and sexually addicted Muslim man comes first in this reform agenda. Thus, "keeping the head open" was taken up as women's emancipation agenda. But they never asked what the Muslim woman who had to be subjected to this reform would say about herself. In this way, women in the colonies became nothing more than a reception site for colonial reform agendas. The hijab has thus pervaded the Western imagination as a cultural symbol justifying colonial transcendence. Certainly, Muslim women's choices have lived in various forms in the Western imagination at different times. The ideas about Muslim women in the Romantic period were different from the Renaissance period.

There is another side to this. Men in colonies who resisted colonial encroachment began to consider women's head coverings as a defence against colonial agendas. They said their culture was women sitting at home. In this way, the burden of culture literally fell on women's heads. This made it easier for men in the colonies to adopt modern clothes and live without the burden of culture, while women in colonized societies became the bearers of culture. So women's clothing in the colonies became part of the conflict between the colonial powers and the colonized men. A particular reading suggests that women in colonized societies were reduced to mere "objects" or "reasons" for men to fight in this struggle. A classic example of this is Algeria, which was a French colony. During the colonial period in Algeria, the French saw the hijab as resistance to their cultural assimilation agenda. Algerians, on the other hand, resisted imperialist domination. This is not to say that these two approaches are the same. Nor is it derogatory in the sense that those who fought against colonialism are oppressors of women.

Orientalism

Orientalism first defined the East as Islamic and distinct from the Christian West. It ignored other religions and cultures of the East and propagated that Islam was the common characteristic of the East. They propagated that Islam can only be understood through Quran and Hadith and their interpretation is still correct. They argued that Islam is only a text and that the practice of Muslims should not be accepted. Thus, they made people believe that hijab is only seen and understood through Islamic principles and the whole world is accepting it in that single way. Thus, erasing the various socio-historical backgrounds of the hijab, its distinctiveness is denied. Second, Islam is a fundamentalist ideology. They argued that the actions of Muslims should be reformed as they are backward. In that, they undertook the historic task of saving a Muslim woman from the hands of a Muslim man as soon as possible. Thus, the wearing of the hijab was judged as a low and degenerate practice and redefined the female condition by making the white Western woman's dress a symbol of global women's clothing freedom.

Liberal Feminism:

Liberal feminist debates are formed in Euro-American countries against gender discrimination and oppression. Liberal upper-class/white women's arguments, which saw all women's issues as one, failed to understand women's issues from different social backgrounds. These are also reflected in discussions related to Muslim women's clothing. Moreover, the influence of the colonial Orientalist discourses mentioned earlier continues to be very evident in such women's arguments. Liberal feminism views Muslim women's clothing in two ways. The first group argues that Muslim women are intelligent and capable, but Muslim men oppress them by wearing the hijab. The second section argues; women who self-select hijab are judged as unintelligent and brainwashed idiots. Liberal feminism reduces Muslim women to either oppressed victims or less capable of thinking, less fortunate human beings.

This book deals not only with perceptions of Muslim women's dress created by colonialism, orientalism and liberal feminism. She also analyses the representation of Muslim women in the public sphere in great detail. They investigate how Muslim women's clothing is represented in the fields of employment, education and other time and country conditions and what are its problems. Most discussions about the representation of the hijab seem to be trapped in two approaches: hijab-liberating or hijab-repressive. Such a dichotomy often fails to fully explain the dilemmas posed by Muslim women's clothing.

In the first half of the twentieth century, many social scientists hypothesized that the increasing privatization of religion in the modern world would lead to a decline in the use of religious symbols in the public sphere. But in contrast to this, the use of the hijab increased in the 1980s and 90s, observes Egyptian Islamic feminist and feminist historian Laila Ahmed. Hijab women who entered the public sphere in this way were generally educated young women from the upper class. They saw the hijab as a gateway from the religious family context into the public sphere. Working outside while wearing a hijab was allowed in some families. In such a situation, Muslim women started wearing hijabs to be model housewives and good workers. Wearing the hijab was read as belonging to the family and religion, as well as facilitating employment outside the home. They mainly overcome two arguments through hijab. One is the secular argument that hijab is a hindrance to women's progress. Two, the specific Islamic approach that women's place is in the world. Through these two observations, Elizabeth Bucar makes very clear the social presence of the Muslim woman who wears the hijab and her agency in society. This approach also challenges the dichotomy of the Hijab being either oppressive or liberating. They see the hijab as a garment that changes women's lives from within the religion/family, in contrast to these oppressive/liberating hijabs.

Workplace conditions that have generally been described as secularly "liberating" have regulated, influenced, and constructed the hijab in many ways. For example, capitalist economic growth in Muslim countries such as Egypt opened many job opportunities. Thus, the Muslim national governments of the post-colonial era promised education and employment to all citizens. Thus, many women started working in various industries and jobs under the government. This created a female working class. There were private capitalists whose men had rams. This is how the government and private capitalists built women's labour forces. Whether or not to wear a hijab around the shoulders is only a reason to protect the interests of male bosses. In short, the secular reading that the workplace as a public space is liberating is highly problematic. The capitalist economic system that controlled the public sphere accepted women in low-wage jobs to their advantage, wearing or not wearing the hijab. This women's emancipation that took place in Egypt was really a "liberation" from the "fences" of religion in the capitalist order.

Second, the book criticizes the use of the hijab in some secular state settings as a cause of discrimination and promotion of barriers. It is mainly contributed to areas where Muslims are in the minority. There are Muslim women who have lost their jobs for not wearing hijab. Secular law courts have ruled that this is an Arab dress and does not violate religious freedom. Thus, they were forced to choose between faith and life, between work and religion. This shows that the secular public sphere "controlled" the access of women in its own way as well as religion.

The modernization that took place in the Muslim world gave great importance to education. The consideration given to the education of girls is noteworthy. As many feminist studies argue, modernizing women is highly problematic. For example, what consumer citizenship really does through education is part of a government agenda. Because of that, modern governments have forced some clothes to protect their interests within the market interest and some have been banned (for example, check the actions of secular governments in countries like Egypt and Turkey).

In a social structure where religion plays a central role, the hijab is seen as a "veil". Religiously speaking, Islam has commanded believers (male and female) to acquire knowledge. But the males and females are also determined to be careful with each other when they grow old. This has led some Muslim communities to assume that the spaces of men and women are different. Some considered the hijab as a "cover" to educate in the modern context. Thus, women were admitted to schools by wearing hijabs. Here the hijab gave the woman the opportunity to gain knowledge in a "restricted" way. But beyond this, by denying entry to a girl who does not wear a hijab, governments like Saudi rule that such women are not entitled to study in the said Muslim countries in any way.

Hijab And Religious/Secular Regimes

Regimes have mandated hijab as part of their unique politics. Iran's American-British-backed autocrat Riza Shah Pahlavi banned the hijab in 1938. Women wearing it were ordered to be arrested if they left the city. The 1979 revolution against the Shah forced the hijab in retaliation. We were able to see that France, Turkey and Belgium, which are said to be democratic secular countries, are also banning the hijab.

The representation of the hijab is its "visibility" in the background of the conflict between the secular state concept and the visibility of religious symbols (specifically the hijab) in the public sphere. In other words, the secular administration began to assume that the use of religious symbols in secular public spaces was a threat to the status quo of the nation's "secular structure". Such secularism has reduced religion to a mere belief in private space. The 1979 Iranian Revolution, the Taliban regime in Afghanistan, the Palestinian Intifada and the events of 9/11 were read as the arrival of Islamic statehood on a global scale. This has worried Western secular nations. Around the same time, girls wearing the hijab began to appear in public places (especially schools) as part of the Muslim migration to the West. This has led to the hijab being easily read as an Islamic religious symbol and thus an adjunct to political Islam. Thus, many secular governments have banned the hijab in schools and public spaces.

This led to conflict between hijabi women and the secular regime. In situations where the hijab is banned in schools, Muslim women have argued that the concept of hijab should be protected under religious freedom. In this way, the secular government expelled the Muslim women who covered their heads from the schools by justifying their side of the liberal women's arguments. Here, secular colleges give freedom to anyone to study without any "mask". But they form "restrictions" so that a Muslim woman can wear the clothes she wants to be seen in college.

Briefly, Bucar shows that there are specific "regulations" around women's bodies and clothing in both religious and secular contexts and that the approach of one as liberating and the other as oppressive is problematic. This book debunks the dominant view that Muslim veiling is caused by women and that it is due to a repressed female identity. In some special situations, Muslim men also forget their heads. For example, the men of the Tuareg Muslim tribe in Morocco forget their heads and faces. Moreover, even women who wear hijab suggest that there are many reasons that motivate them to do so.

Hijab as a choice has many interesting historical contexts. Hijab was seen by Egyptian secular feminist 'Huda Sharavi' as a defence against imperial power during British colonialism. Later, when the country became independent, the hijab was abandoned. At the same time, Islamist women who were fighting against French colonialism in Algeria ditched the hijab and disguised themselves as European women to smuggle weapons through the French checkpoints. Thus, women use hijab as a choice in many ways. Those are areas of study that require a lot of close reading and special contextualization.

Hijab has many meanings in many situations. It cannot be simplified in the sense of either liberation or oppression. Sometimes a personal choice can be surrender in a structural sense in another situation. Conversely, an apparent capitulation may also create a large opening in a structural sense. Or as 'Saba Mahmud' observes, oppression/liberation can be another way of working/living that makes them irrelevant. Discussions about the hijab are often framed through the lens of liberation/oppression. Only the hijab, the garment of the oppressed woman, and the Muslim woman standing with her face down in a single way are seen in such analyses. Elizabeth Bucar tries to say that 'the hijab is part of a symbolic system that produces multiple meanings. The prevalence of hijab in different socio-cultural political contexts is quite different.

Even Muslim women living in the same social environment (same houses/offices/workplaces/educational institutions/streets/places of worship) have different opinions about the hijab. Thus, this book tells us that the hijab is not an issue that can be easily manipulated by comment, but a very micro-political garment. This book underlines that the modern-secular logic that the hijab can be easily defined does not take into account the extremely pluralistic approach of the Islamic community on this issue. From medieval male Islamic scholars to Islamic feminists Amina Wadud, and Laila Ahmad, this book shows that they hold different opinions about the hijab and that these define Muslims as a group in many ways. Moreover, this book demonstrates that the secular rationale for policing the hijab is not entirely immune to colonial-orientalist stereotypes about Muslims.

CHAPTER XXII

Forgotten Matriarchal Islam In India

Matriarchy was widely practiced till mid twentieth century by Muslims in parts of North Malabar and in Travancore princely State. According to matriarchal system, a local accretion to Islam from Hindu ruling class, Islam was practiced giving prominence to women, in variation with patriarchal understanding of Islam across the Islamic world, matriarchal practices have wane, except in some pockets of African coastal regions and Indonesia and Lakshadweep, significantly denting women-oriented Islamic reading of scriptures.

While the tradition has been extinct in Malabar, some practices are still followed. For example, after marriage husband lives at wife's house. And the familial expenses are the concern of matriarchal heads of family members too. The colonial changes in Islamic law and shift to nuclear family were the prime movers behind this shift. But when the issue of Muslim women's rights in Islam is hotly contested, understanding of matriarchal understanding of Islam is contemporaneous.

According to anthropologists, in Kerala matriarchy was practiced by people of Sangham Age (BC 5 – AD 5), which continued till twentieth century with occasional modifications. Sambamdham Practice (this practice stipulated marriage of only elder son while other siblings condemned to practice akin to today's living-in relationship, where women in the relation had sexual freedom and children were known to be children of women in the relationship) among Hindus endured the tradition. Matriarchal lineage is considered to be one essential pillar of caste system in South India.

According to this tradition, joint family will be headed by uncles of female members. The family wealth will be enjoyed through the lineage of women members. More preference used to be accorded to siblings of sisters while male members lived off the free allowances without any claim on property. Property will not be divided, but owned commonly with free claim to shared daily allowance. The self-made properties of male members will be given to his sisters' children, while his own children will not have claim over this. This tradition became popular in Kerala by tenth century. Zamorins, Chrirakkal ruling families adopted this tradition.

Anthropologists equates this practice to pre-Islamic '*Muta*' (temporary marriage) of Arabia. In this pre-fixed marriage contract, women had right to maintenance and freedom to leave the relationship unilaterally. With Arabs crisscrossing the world for mercantile purposes, they practiced this kind of marriage wherever they went. In Kerala, local rulers promoted such marriage. Arabs who followed monsoon stayed at Kerala for months. 'Mappila' community grew out of these inter-racial marriages. Zamorin supported such short-term alliances and hence it became popular among Muslims of North Malabar. Besides, close cultural bonhomie between Hindu Nairs and Muslims during united fight against Portuguese naturally gave the matriarchal practices more acceptance. The united spirit faltered the efforts of Portuguese to subjugate people of Kerala.

Matriarchal tradition among Mappila Muslims is a good example of 'localization of Islam'. at Kozhikode and Ponnani, partial practices of matriarchy were followed. While inheritance division was given according to Quranic instructions, in other practices it deviated from popular Islamic forms. Rights of wife, maintenance of family, identity and local rituals were innovative and women enjoyed singular agency and independence. The only Muslim ruling kingdom of Kerala, Arakkal Kudumbam, followed this tradition. In the family, rulership passed over through matriarchal lineage. After the death of a ruler, children of sister claimed the right to throne.

Historians are dissenters about the origin of the practice. The practice became Islamic either after matriarchal Hindu families accepted Islam and continued local customs or Arab merchants employed this marital alliance. By the time colonialism came, matriarchal Islam was practiced in many places including Memons of Gujarat, Labbas of Tamil Nadu and Mappilas of Malabar.

Colonialism And New Ethics Of Law

Colonial modernity was totally alien to Indian traditions and rooted in western Biblical foundations. Liberty to women and sexual independence to female were anathema in colonial legal mooring. The Islamic reform movement motivated by colonial ideas, revolted against this tradition. Muslim reformers hollered against this practice unfound in Islamic scriptures. They were following colonial idea of Islam being monolithic and Arabian-centred. The severe casualty in colonial Islamic modernization was the sheening off local practices (urf) from legal recognition. Sayyid Sanaullah Makti Thangal (1847-1912) crusaded against this practice in Kerala and later took up by eminent reformers.

In British Legislative Assemblies, discussions were held about the issue. By 1937 Shariat Act, matriarchal traditions were invalidated across India. But 1937 law was not applicable to agricultural land. So, K.M Seethi Sahib brought amendment to the law by including agricultural land in Shariat domain. In Cochin principality, law was brought banning the practice in 1933.

In Madras Assembly Mappila Inheritance Law was enacted in 1918. As per the new law, the practice of using Waqf instruments to give property for women in the family was forfeited. By 1939 Madras Act, property division was channelized through paternal lineage, thus ending the institution of matriarchal Islam in Malabar. By 1976, the practice was outlawed among Hindus too. The practice crumbled entirely by 1960s and only vestiges of the former tradition is found now, with ritual skeletons littered here and there.

The practice has to be renegotiated within the broader perspective of changing debates of Muslim women's rights in Islam. Once denounced, this Islamic local practice is notable for its gender sensitive approach. It gives immense agency to women in matters of marriage and sexual choices. Women are empowered through financial securities and gives better position in family set-up. The system abolished under reformation spirit needs retrospection to accommodate emerging women concern within religious framework.

CHAPTER XXIII

Nikah Halala Has No Legitimacy In Islam

The BBC recently published a report on online services operating in London to facilitate the reunification of couples who have ended their marriages due to triple talaq. It appeared in the online media at a time when issues related to Muslim women, including Mutwalaq, were being actively debated. It is natural that anti-Muslims and hypocritical women defenders used the said report as a stick to beat Islam. The BBC recently published a report on online services operating in London to facilitate the reunification of couples who have ended their marriages due to triple talaq. Issues related to Muslim women including Mutwalaq are actively appeared in the online media while it was being debated. It is natural that anti-Muslims and hypocritical women defenders used the said report as a stick to beat Islam. The method of these services is to charge lakhs of rupees and marry the divorced women in the name of Nikah Halala and then give them to others and use them sexually. Debates regarding the status of Muslim women are favourite subjects of critics of Islam. Ignorance and misunderstanding of religious rules are behind such criticisms. Triple talaq and related procedures are a much debated topic among the group

He also felt sad because of the divorce. And with that came the thought of a reunion. That's when I came to know about the agencies working for Nikah Halala. But she came to a new decision when she heard stories of the financial and sexual exploitation of many divorcees. He is not ready to save his marriage by sharing a bed with strangers. Debates regarding the status of Muslim women are favourite subjects of critics of Islam. Ignorance and misunderstanding of religious rules are behind such criticisms. Triple talaq and related procedures are a much-debated topic among the group. The law related to this has been declared in the 230th verse of the Holy Qur'an Surat al-Baqarah. " The divorcee can be taken back without a new Nikah if it is during the initiation period and if it is later through Nikah if the relationship is separated by one or two Talaqs. This concession is not applicable to those availing one more chance.

For them to be reunited, someone else must marry her and have intercourse with her and divorce her" is the meaning of the said verse. An extremely difficult situation that existed in the early days of Islam was rectified by this. Or, no matter how many times a woman was divorced, it was a practice that she could be taken back during initiation. Many used the said method as part of torturing their wives. For them to be reunited, someone else must marry her and have intercourse with her and divorce her" is the meaning of the said verse. An extremely difficult situation that existed in the early days of Islam was rectified by this. Or, no matter how many times a woman was divorced, it was a practice that she could be taken back during initiation. Many used the said method as part of torturing their wives. For them to be reunited, someone else must marry her and have intercourse with her and divorce her" is the meaning of the said verse. An extremely difficult situation that existed in the early days of Islam was rectified by this. Or, no matter how many times a woman was divorced, it was a practice that she could be taken back during initiation. Many used the said method as part of torturing their wives.

Among them were those who made it difficult for women to divorce and take back by swearing that I would not associate with them or leave them. Islam does not encourage the termination of a divorce, which is possible after the initiation period of a single talaq, by taking full advantage of the prescribed opportunities. On the contrary, the order of Islam is to stay away from it as much as possible and continue the relationship if possible. This is why strict procedures have been put forward in connection with the recitation of triple talaq. Or she who has been recited three Twalaqs to her status as a wife if you want to come back, you have to marry someone else and share a bed. There is no doubt that this law prevents a self-righteous man from reciting triple talaq. Marrying a woman who has been pronounced triple talaq by another person should not be considered as a divorce. On the contrary, marriage with interest is what the Qur'an means. Moreover, Karahat helps those who bypass simple methods of divorce to remarry. The law of Islam states that the marriage itself is not valid if the said Nikah comes with the condition of divorce. By that means remarriage is also not allowed for the first. But having such an understanding before the Nikah ceremony does not affect the validity.

The Holy Prophet insulted the one who married to facilitate the first husband as a 'rent-seeker'. It has been mentioned in the scriptures that there is a curse for such people and for whom they marry. There are those who believe that a second marriage is enough to remarry a woman who has been pronounced three talaqs. Saying that they should also have sex is interpreted by such people as an encouragement to exploit the woman. But it was through the actions of the prophets that the matter was established. Or the wife of Rifaa (ra) married Abdurrahman bin Zubayr (ra) after three talaqs were pronounced. When she expressed her desire to go back to her first husband before intercourse, the Holy Prophet forbade it and clarified that it is not possible to go back before intercourse. Criticisms against triple talaq and follow-up procedures will cease if it is understood that such logical goals are pre-set and systematic.

It goes without saying that the Nikah Halala services mentioned above are not related to religion and are aimed at economic sexual exploitation. Those who go ahead with such heinous ways are not defenders of religious values or those who want to keep the marital relationship intact.

CHAPTER XXIV

The Essential Religious Practices Test and Islamic Law in India

The Essential Religious Practices (ERP) test has become a pivotal tool in Indian jurisprudence, especially in matters relating to religious freedoms and practices. This doctrine determines whether a particular religious practice is fundamental to a religion, thus deserving of constitutional protection. The ERP test has profoundly impacted various cases, including those concerning Islamic law. This article delves into the intricacies of the ERP test, its implications on Islamic law in India, and the recent Supreme Court verdict on the Muslim Women's Right to Maintenance.

The Genesis Of The Essential Religious Practices Test

The ERP test emerged from a series of judicial decisions aimed at balancing the freedom of religion with the state's responsibility to uphold public order, morality, and health. The test's origins can be traced to the landmark 1954 Supreme Court judgment in The Commissioner, Hindu Religious Endowments, Madras v. Shri Lakshmindra Thirtha Swamiar of Shirur Mutt. In this case, the Court held that only those practices integral to a religion are protected under Articles 25 and 26 of the Indian Constitution. This test was designed to prevent the protection of superfluous religious practices that could conflict with public order and social welfare.

Application Of The ERP Test In Indian Courts

Over the decades, the ERP test has been applied in numerous cases, shaping the legal landscape of religious practices in India. Courts have used this test to evaluate the essentiality of various practices, often leading to contentious judgments. For instance, the Karnataka High Court's decision to uphold the ban on hijabs in educational institutions relied heavily on the ERP test. The Court ruled that wearing a hijab is not an essential practice of Islam, thus not warranting constitutional protection. This decision was met with significant criticism and is currently under review by the Supreme Court.

The ERP test has faced substantial criticism from scholars, legal experts, and religious communities. One primary concern is that the judiciary, rather than the religious communities themselves, determines what constitutes an essential practice. This judicial overreach can lead to the homogenization of diverse religious practices and may lack the nuanced understanding required to interpret complex religious doctrines. Moreover, critics argue that the ERP test may inadvertently legitimize oppressive practices under the guise of religious essentiality. This potential for misuse underscores the need for a more comprehensive approach to evaluating religious practices, considering broader human rights implications and the evolving social context.

The Hijab Ban Controversy

The hijab ban controversy in Karnataka highlights the contentious nature of the ERP test. The Karnataka High Court's ruling that hijabs are not essential to Islam sparked widespread debate. Critics of the decision argued that the Court's focus on the ERP test overshadowed more fundamental rights, such as equality, personal liberty, and freedom of expression. The Supreme Court's review of this case is expected to address these broader constitutional questions, potentially redefining the application of the ERP test in future cases.

The Supreme Court's Verdict On The Muslim Women's Right To Maintenance

In a landmark judgment, the Supreme Court recently upheld the right of divorced Muslim women to maintenance beyond the *Iddat* period under Section 125 of the Criminal Procedure Code (CrPC). This verdict reinforces the Court's commitment to protecting individual rights within the framework of Islamic law. The judgment clarifies that divorced Muslim women are entitled to maintenance until they remarry or become self-sufficient, aligning with the principles of justice and equality enshrined in the Constitution.

This decision has significant implications for the interpretation of Islamic law in India. It demonstrates the judiciary's willingness to reinterpret religious laws in light of constitutional values, ensuring that personal laws do not infringe upon fundamental rights. The verdict also reflects a broader trend towards gender justice and empowerment within the Indian legal system.

Implications Of The Verdict On Islamic Law

The Supreme Court's verdict on the Muslim Women's Right to Maintenance marks a progressive step towards ensuring gender justice in Islamic law. By upholding the maintenance rights of divorced Muslim women, the Court has reinforced the constitutional mandate of equality and non-discrimination. This decision is likely to influence future interpretations of personal laws, encouraging a more rights-based approach to religious practices.

Furthermore, this judgment highlights the evolving nature of Islamic law in India, adapting to contemporary social and legal standards. It underscores the importance of interpreting religious laws in a manner that harmonizes with the broader constitutional framework, ensuring that individual rights are not compromised.

The Future Of The ERP Test And Islamic Law In India

The ongoing debates and judicial reviews surrounding the ERP test indicate that its application in Indian jurisprudence is far from settled. The Supreme Court's forthcoming decision on the hijab ban case will likely have far-reaching implications for the ERP doctrine and its role in evaluating religious practices. This case presents an opportunity for the Court to reassess the ERP test's relevance and effectiveness, potentially paving the way for a more holistic approach to religious freedom and individual rights.

In the context of Islamic law, the Supreme Court's recent judgments reflect a trend towards balancing religious practices with constitutional values. As India continues to navigate the complex interplay between religious freedom and individual rights, the judiciary's role in interpreting and shaping these principles will be crucial. The ERP test, while contentious, remains a vital tool in this process, necessitating careful and nuanced application to uphold justice and equality.

The Essential Religious Practices test has profoundly influenced the legal landscape of religious practices in India, particularly concerning Islamic law. While the test aims to balance religious freedom with public order and social welfare, its application has sparked significant debate and criticism. The ongoing hijab ban controversy and the recent Supreme Court verdict on the Muslim Women's Right to Maintenance underscore the complexities and challenges of applying the ERP test in a diverse and pluralistic society.

As the judiciary continues to interpret and refine the ERP doctrine, it is imperative to consider the broader implications of these decisions on individual rights and social justice. The evolving nature of Islamic law in India reflects a commitment to aligning religious practices with constitutional values, ensuring that personal laws do not infringe upon fundamental rights. The future of the ERP test will likely shape the contours of religious freedom and individual rights in India, necessitating a balanced and inclusive approach to justice.

By examining the ERP test's application and its impact on Islamic law, this article highlights the ongoing legal and social discourse surrounding religious practices in India. The judiciary's role in interpreting and shaping these principles will be crucial in ensuring that religious freedom and individual rights are upheld in a manner that reflects the values of justice, equality, and non-discrimination enshrined in the Indian Constitution.

CHAPTER XXV

The Complex Route To Gender Equality For Muslim Women In Divorce And Alimony Issues

The Shah Bano case in the 1980s brought significant attention to the plight of Muslim women seeking alimony post-divorce. Shah Bano Begum, after being divorced at 62 following a 42-year marriage, sought financial support from her husband. The Supreme Court initially ruled in her favour, advocating for alimony under Section 125 of the Code of Criminal Procedure (CrPC), which applies universally across religious denominations. However, the subsequent political backlash led to the enactment of the Muslim Women (Protection of Rights on Divorce) Act, 1986, effectively limiting Muslim women's alimony rights to the iddah period.

A five-judge bench headed by Chief Justice YV Chandrachud, father of today's Chief Justice DY Chandrachud, changed even the political history of India by Mohd. Ahmed Khan v. Judgment in the case of Shah Bano Begum (1985 SCR (3) 844). In 1978, his 62-year-old wife, Shah Bano, married her husband, Adv. A suit was filed for recovery of costs from Muhammad Ahmad Khan. They lived together for 43 years. The husband went all the way to the Supreme Court to establish the argument that he is entitled to receive expenses only during the Iddah period (three lunar months) as per Islamic Shariah as he is divorced. Rejecting all his arguments, the Supreme Court strictly held that Shah Banu Begum is entitled to costs under CrPC 125. Not only did it place secular law above religious law, but it was fair to ensure the protection of Muslim women in a secular country.

Against that ruling, religious leaders organised Sharia protection rallies in all parts of the country. Religious leaders and religious politicians joined them and organised an agitation against the humanitarian decision to pay expenses to the woman who lived with them for 43 years. Prime Minister Shri Rajiv Gandhi surrendered to the fundamentalists of Islam. The Muslim Divorcee Protection Act 1986 was passed to override the Supreme Court ruling. Rajiv Gandhi's Law Minister Ashok Sen introduced the bill in the House that day. The Muslim unification of that time and the creation of laws that favoured religious fundamentalists led to the strengthening of Hindutva politics. They campaigned on a large scale against this "Muslim Appeasement Policy". Ram temple stone-laying and Ayodhya were burnt.

The 1986 Act is an unjust law that was achieved by subjugating the political leadership by men standing united against Muslim women in independent India. Although the Act of 1986 had many other features, the way it came about was enough to determine the political future of India and history recorded that religious supremacy subjugated political leadership. The boost it gave to Hindutva politics was not insignificant. This legislative move was seen as a political strategy to appease the Muslim community while ostensibly adhering to Shariah law. Under Shariah, maintenance is provided only during the iddah, after which responsibility shifts to family heirs or the state Waqf Board. This framework, however, often leaves divorced women in prolonged legal battles for sustenance, ignoring their health, age, and living conditions.

Recent Judicial Developments

Recent court rulings, including the 2024 Supreme Court decision, reaffirm that Section 125 of the CrPC applies to all religious groups, highlighting the constitutional imperative for uniformity and non-discrimination. The judgment allows Muslim women to claim alimony beyond the Iddah period, challenging previous interpretations that restricted such claims to either Shariah or civil law provisions. This marks a significant shift towards aligning religious practices with constitutional values, ensuring equitable outcomes for all Indian citizens.

In this case, the Supreme Court has reiterated that the judgment rendering the Shariat Application Act, 1937, inapplicable is fair. In 2010 and 2024, the Supreme Court issued the same verdict as in 1985. But to override the 1985 judgment, the government made a law in 1986 for male subjects. The Supreme Court has issued three important judgments in a way that undermines the essence of the 86 Act. But the fundamental change from 1985 to 2024 is that the religious clergy or religious politicians are not ready to question the justice of the Supreme Court. This shows that even when the religious priesthood takes anti-women positions, the Ummah rejects it. It is also hopeful that no organization like the Congress Party, which led the drafting of the law in 1986, or the Jamaat-e-Islami, Muslim League, Muslim Personal Law Board, etc., which supported it at that time, is taking a position against the 2024 ruling.

Mehr, or dower, is a traditional Islamic marriage provision meant to secure a woman's financial future. However, in India, the amount often remains meager, inadequate for long-term support post-divorce. This disparity complicates the debate over whether Shariah provisions suffice for modern financial realities. The courts have ruled that Muslim women can seek additional alimony under CrPC 125, reflecting a growing recognition of the need for comprehensive financial security measures post-divorce.

Societal and Cultural Challenges

While legal advancements are crucial, societal attitudes and entrenched cultural norms continue to pose significant challenges. Education and advocacy are essential to shift public perceptions and foster a more inclusive legal framework that respects and protects women's rights across all communities. Ensuring that men recognize and act on the financial dependence of homemakers is also vital for gender justice and economic empowerment.

If the figures after the 1980s are revised, it can be seen that the rate of polygamy is coming down sharply, and it will be realized at the practical level that the Muslim community is a society that is turning its back on the right of polygamy. However the political leadership is taking the approach of supporting the Muslim clergy to insist on a right that is completely useless. According to Section 494 of the Indian Penal Code, only one marriage is allowed for a person. This section is meant to punish a person who has married more than once. Section 82 of the Indian Penal Code, which came into force on July 1, is similar.

The journey toward gender equality for Muslim women in matters of divorce and alimony is fraught with complexities rooted in legal interpretations, cultural traditions, and political considerations. As legal precedents evolve, so too must societal attitudes and legislative frameworks to foster a more just and inclusive society for all Indians. The judiciary's role in upholding these principles is paramount in ensuring that every woman can assert her rights with dignity and equality under the law.

Conclusion

The interplay between Islamic Sharia and the Indian Constitution represents a complex and evolving relationship that has shaped the socio-legal landscape of India since its independence. As India is a secular state with a diverse population, the coexistence of different legal systems, particularly the personal laws governed by religious doctrines, has been both a source of harmony and contention. The book "Sharia Meets Constitution: Islamic Sharia in Independent India" delves into this intricate relationship, exploring the historical roots, legal frameworks, societal impacts, and future prospects of Islamic Sharia within the broader constitutional structure of India.

In examining the historical trajectory, it is evident that the legacy of Islamic jurisprudence in India predates the colonial era. The Mughal Empire, with its sophisticated legal system, laid the foundation for the application of Sharia in matters of personal law among Muslims. However, the advent of British colonial rule brought about significant changes. The British, while retaining certain elements of Sharia in the personal law domain, also introduced their legal codes, leading to a dual legal system that persisted into the post-independence era. This duality created a unique challenge for independent India, which was now tasked with the monumental responsibility of drafting a constitution that would uphold secular values while respecting the religious diversity of its citizens.

The Constitution of India, adopted in 1950, is a testament to the nation's commitment to secularism, democracy, and the protection of fundamental rights. It enshrines the principles of equality, non-discrimination, and religious freedom, all of which are pivotal in ensuring that India remains a pluralistic society. However, the inclusion of personal laws based on religious doctrines, including Islamic Sharia, within the legal framework presents a paradox. On one hand, it allows religious communities to preserve their identities and traditions; on the other hand, it raises questions about the uniformity of rights and the potential for conflict with constitutional principles.

The book meticulously explores the legal provisions and judicial interpretations that have shaped the application of Sharia in independent India. The Muslim Personal Law (Shariat) Application Act of 1937, which governs marriage, divorce, inheritance, and other personal matters for Muslims, is a focal point of this discussion. This Act is often at the center of debates on whether personal laws should be reformed to align with constitutional values or whether they should be preserved as a means of protecting religious freedom. The Judiciary, through its interpretations and rulings, has played a crucial role in navigating these debates, balancing the need to uphold constitutional rights while respecting religious autonomy.

One of the significant themes of the book is the tension between religious freedom and gender justice. Islamic Sharia, like other religious legal systems, has been critiqued for perpetuating gender inequalities, particularly in areas such as marriage, divorce, and inheritance. The book delves into landmark cases where the Supreme Court of India has had to adjudicate on matters involving the rights of Muslim women. The Shah Bano case of 1985, where the Court upheld the right of a divorced Muslim woman to maintenance under secular law, sparked a nationwide debate on the need for a uniform civil code versus the protection of religious laws. This case, and others like it, highlight the ongoing struggle to reconcile the demands of gender justice with the rights of religious communities to govern their affairs according to their beliefs.

The concept of a uniform civil code, as envisaged by Article 44 of the Indian Constitution, is another critical area of exploration in the book. The uniform civil code represents the idea of having a common set of laws governing personal matters for all citizens, irrespective of their religion. While this concept aligns with the constitutional values of equality and non-discrimination, it has been met with resistance from various religious communities, including Muslims, who view it as an infringement on their religious rights. The book provides a nuanced analysis of the debates surrounding the uniform civil code, considering the perspectives of different stakeholders and the implications for India's secular fabric.

In addition to the legal and constitutional dimensions, the book also delves into the societal impact of the interaction between Sharia and the Constitution. The role of religious and political leaders, community organizations, and civil society in shaping public opinion and influencing policy decisions is examined in detail. The book highlights the divergent views within the Muslim community itself, with some advocating for the preservation of Sharia as a means of protecting religious identity, while others call for reform to ensure that Islamic law is in harmony with contemporary values of justice and equality.

The book also addresses the broader implications of the Sharia-Constitution nexus for India's secularism. Secularism in India, as interpreted by the Constitution, is not about the strict separation of religion and state, but rather the equal treatment of all religions by the state. This model of secularism has allowed for the coexistence of multiple religious legal systems, but it has also led to challenges in ensuring that all citizens enjoy equal rights and protections under the law. The book argues that the future of India's secularism depends on how effectively it can manage the relationship between religious laws and constitutional principles, ensuring that neither is compromised in the pursuit of justice and equity.

Looking ahead, the book suggests that the relationship between Sharia and the Constitution will continue to evolve in response to changing societal dynamics, legal developments, and global trends. The rise of Islamic reform movements, the influence of international human rights norms, and the growing demand for gender justice are likely to shape the future discourse on the role of Sharia in India. The book calls for a continuous dialogue between religious scholars, legal experts, policymakers, and civil society to find ways to harmonize Sharia with constitutional values, ensuring that the rights of all citizens are protected while respecting religious diversity.

In conclusion, the book offers a comprehensive and insightful analysis of the complex and multifaceted relationship between Islamic Sharia and the Indian Constitution. It highlights the challenges and opportunities that arise from this relationship, emphasizing the need for a balanced approach that upholds the principles of justice, equality, and religious freedom. As India continues to navigate its path as a secular democracy with a pluralistic society, the interplay between Sharia and the Constitution will remain a critical area of engagement, requiring thoughtful consideration and dialogue among all stakeholders. The book serves as a valuable resource for understanding this intricate relationship and its implications for the future of India's legal and constitutional landscape.

Further Reading

- Historical development

Al-Azami, M. M. (1996) On Schacht's Origins of Muhammadan Jurisprudence, Oxford: OCIS.

Coulson, N. J. (1964) A History of Islamic Law, Edinburgh: Edinburgh University Press.

Faruqi, M. Y. (2007) Development of Usul al-Fiqh: An Early Historical Perspective, New Delhi: Adam Publishers & Distributors.

Schacht, J. (1950) The Origins of Muhammadan Jurisprudence, Oxford: The Clarendon Press.

- The nature of Islamic law

Baderin, M. A. (2009) 'Islamic Legal Theory in Context' in Baderin, M.A. (ed.) Islamic Legal Theory, Vol. 1, Aldershot: Ashgate Publishing, pp. xi–xxxvii.

Dupret, B. (2018) What is the Shari'a? London: C. Hurst & Co. (Publishers) Ltd.

Hallaq, W. B. (1997) A History of Islamic Legal Theories, Cambridge: Cambridge University Press.

Schacht, J. (1964) An Introduction to Islamic Law, Oxford: The Clarendon Press.

- Theory, scope, and practice

Kamali, M. H. (2003) Principles of Islamic Jurisprudence, 3rd edn, Cambridge: Islamic Texts Society.

Khadduri, M. (1987) al-Shāfiʿī's Risāla: Treatise on the Foundations of Islamic Jurisprudence, Cambridge: Islamic Texts Society.

Nyazee, I. A. (2016) Outlines of Islamic Jurisprudence, 6th edn, Islamabad: Centre for Excellence in Research.

Qadri, A. A. (1986) Islamic Jurisprudence in the Modern World, Delhi: Taj Company.

• Family law

'Abd al 'Atī, H. (1977) The Family Structure in Islam, Indianapolis: American Trust Publications.
Mansoori, M. T. (2012) Family Law in Islam: Theory and Application, Islamabad: Shariah Academy, International Islamic University.
Nasir, J. J. (2009) The Islamic Law of Personal Status, 3rd revised and updated edn, Leiden: Brill.
Welchman, L. (2014) Women and Muslim Family Laws in Arab States: A Comparative Overview of Textual Development and Advocacy, Amsterdam: Amsterdam University Press.

• Law of inheritance

Coulson, N. J. (1971) Succession in Muslim Family Law, Cambridge: Cambridge University Press.
Hussain, A. (2005) The Islamic Law of Succession, Riyadh: Maktaba Darussalam.
Khan, H. (2007) The Islamic Law of Inheritance, Oxford: Oxford University Press.

• Law of financial transactions

Aldohi, A. K. (2011) The Legal and Regulatory Aspects of Islamic Banking: A Comparative Look at the United Kingdom and Malaysia, London: Routledge.
Mansuri, M. T. (2006) Islamic Law of Contracts and Business Transactions, New Delhi: Adam Publishers and Distributors.
Usmani, M. T. (2010) An Introduction to Islamic Finance, Karachi: Quranic Studies Publishers.
Visser, H. (2009) Islamic Finance: Principles and Practice,

Cheltenham: Edward Elgar.

- Penal law

Baderin, M. A. (2006) 'Effective Legal Representation in "Sharī'ah" Courts as a Means of Addressing Human Rights Concerns in the Islamic Criminal Justice System of Muslim States', 11 Yearbook of Islamic and Middle Eastern Law, 2004–2005, pp. 135–67.
Bassiouni, M. C. (ed.) (1982) The Islamic Criminal Justice System, New York: Oceania Publications.
Kamali, M. H. (2019) Crime and Punishment in Islamic Law: A Fresh Interpretation, Oxford: Oxford University Press.
Peters, R. (2006) Crime and Punishment in Islamic Law, Cambridge: Cambridge University Press.

- International law (al-siyar)

Baderin, M. A. (2003) International Human Rights and Islamic Law, Oxford: OUP.
Bsoul, L. B. (2008) International Treaties (Mu'āhadāt) in Islam: Theory and Practice in the Light of Islamic International Law (Siyar) According to Orthodox Schools, Lanham, MD: University Press of America.
Hamidullah, M. (1977) The Muslim Conduct of State, 7th edn, Lahore: Muhammad Ashraf Publishers.
Khadduri, M. (1966) The Islamic Law of Nations: Shaybani's Siyar, Baltimore: Johns Hopkins Press.

- Administration of justice

Al-Alwani, T. J. (1995) 'The Rights of the Accused in Islam', 10 Arab Law Quarterly, No. 4, pp. 3–16.
Anderson, J. N. D. (1949) 'Muslim Procedure and Evidence', 1 Journal of African Administration, pp. 123–9, 176–83.

Anwarullah (1999) Principles of Evidence in Islam, Kuala Lumpur: A. S. Noordeen.

Azad, G. M. (1987) Judicial System of Islam, Islamabad: Islamic Research Institute.

- The future of Islamic law

Abou El Fadl, K. (2005) The Great Theft: Wrestling Islam from the Extremists, New York: HarperCollins Publishers.

Ali, S. S. (2016) Modern Challenges to Islamic Law, Cambridge: Cambridge University Press.

Black, A., Esmaeili, H., and Hosen, N. (2013) Modern Perspectives on Islamic Law, Cheltenham: Edward Elgar Publishing Ltd.

Hallaq, W. B. (2014) The Impossible State: Islam, Politics, and Modernity's Moral Predicament, Columbia: Columbia University Press.